The Hard-Pressed Researcher

A research handbook for
the caring professions

Second Edition

Anne Edwards and Robin Talbot

Prentice
Hall

An imprint of Pearson Education

Harlow, England · London · New York · Reading, Massachusetts · San Francisco
Toronto · Don Mills, Ontario · Sydney · Tokyo · Singapore · Hong Kong · Seoul
Taipei · Cape Town · Madrid · Mexico City · Amsterdam · Munich · Paris · Milan

Pearson Education Limited
Edinburgh Gate
Harlow
Essex CM20 2JE
England

and Associated Companies throughout the world

Visit us on the World Wide Web at:
www.pearsoned.co.uk

First published 1994
Second edition 1999

ISBN 0 582 36972 X

British Library Cataloguing-in-Publication Data
A catalogue record for this book is available from the British Library

Library of Congress Cataloging-in-Publication Data
Edwards, Anne, 1946–
    The hard-pressed researcher: a research handbook for the caring
professions/
    Anne Edwards and Robin Talbot.
        p. cm.
    Includes bibliographical references and index.
    ISBN 0–582–36972–X
    1. Nursing—Research. 2. Social service—Research.
    I. Talbot, Robin, 1952– . II. Title.
    RT81.5.E38 1994
    001.4–dc20   94–68
                                                                CIP

Set by 43 in 10/12pt New Baskerville
Printed and bound by CPI Antony Rowe, Eastbourne

Contents

Acknowledgements

Above all we thank the students and practitioners with whom we have worked over the last twenty years. They have consistently made their needs clear and have consequently guided our selection of topics for this text.

Finally our thanks go to our families which have always shown the tolerance demanded of the families and friends of practitioner researchers.

Introduction

This book has been written as a guide for the thousands of practitioners who are undertaking research in the settings in which they are training or working. Practitioner research usually involves researching while also working and juggling the other interests and commitments that make life worthwhile. These days, to be working or training in the fields of health, social services, community work and education is demanding enough without the added pressure of a research project.

With this in mind we have put together a text which attempts to answer the questions raised by the hard-pressed researchers we work with. We are grateful to them for their relentless no-nonsense queries and their impact on our own thinking. At the same time we recognise that the well-informed practitioners we know do not want to shirk some of the more fundamental questions that help them shape their projects. Consequently we have not avoided some of the more complex questions about the nature of the research enquiry. This is essentially a practical and informative text. We hope that it does not veer into over-simplification, but allows you to trace the paths which are best suited to the enquiries you wish to make. At the end of each chapter we have made some suggestions for further reading in order to introduce readers to some specialist work.

Because research can be seen as a quest and the research process as a pathway, this has been a difficult book to write. Chapter 1, entitled 'Finding direction', aims at helping you to determine the research question you will be asking. But the question cannot be finalised without knowledge of the implications of any type of question. 'Will my question demand large-scale survey data or a small-scale case study enquiry?' is an entirely proper question to ask as you select the path you will take. Consequently, although specific chapters deal with clearly named issues in depth, there is some cross-referencing throughout and advance frameworks are offered in the early part of the book. This is particularly the case in Chapter 1. But the main messages in that chapter are: be selfish, be orderly and be aware that you might become the obsessive researcher.

The second chapter gives you the practical guidance you will need as you develop your study skills. It includes making notes, reading research reports and library use. It may be read alongside aspects of Chapter 7, which gives guidance in writing up a dissertation. Chapter 7 focuses largely on dissertations, but throughout the rest of the book the information given is as appropriate to non-award-bearing research as it is to research which is geared to an academic award.

Chapters 3, 4 and 5 look, in turn, at the design of a study, action research and the methods that might be used in a research enquiry. They address in practical detail how you might tackle a research project and the information collection methods best suited to practitioner research.

Often the most difficult aspect of research is the analysis of the information that has been gathered. It is frequently the weakest element in submitted projects. Chapter 6 takes you through aspects of the analysis process and relates methods of analysis to the methods of data collection given in Chapter 5.

The final chapter guides you through the conventions associated with the presentation of your research. It concludes with the suggestion that you should consider the publication of your research. It is a suggestion which we hope will be taken seriously.

The book concludes with a glossary of technical terms, as research, like any other field of study, has its own shorthand.

The most challenging aspect of this book has been the tracing, and often subsequent ignoring, of the boundaries that have been erected around modes of research. Our own research experience tells us that case study work can be incorporated into research designs that are largely concerned with numerical data, that action research draws eclectically on all kinds of data-collection strategies, and that you cannot ignore the importance of changing context in the most carefully controlled experimental designs. We have tried to present, in an open way, a wide range of alternative research strategies, but doubtless our comments on some aspects of practitioner research will have been informed by our own experiences and those of our students.

Indeed, as may be evident in the text, we each operate as researchers in very different ways. Yet we have worked together regularly in supporting student research and found our differences to be fruitful. In this volume Anne Edwards is largely responsible for Chapters 1, 4, 5 and 7 and Robin Talbot for Chapters 2, 3 and 6. We have, however, read and contributed to each others' chapters and jointly remain culpable for any flaws.

We are both enthusiastic researchers who regard the exercise as one way of keeping sane while the contexts in which we work respond dramatically to change. We hope that our enthusiasm is catching.

Chapter 1

Finding direction

Why do research?

This question may well come to mind on more than one occasion over the period of your research project. It is, therefore, as well to be sure of what can be gained from undertaking a research-based study or from simply taking a research perspective in your pursuit of a deeper understanding of an initiative or situation at work. If you have embarked on the research quest in order to receive a qualification, that may seem a sufficient end in itself. But, increasingly, employers are seeing the advantages that research enquiries bring to organisational development and are harnessing the professional development of employees to wider institutional, team or corporate ends. It is therefore likely that most researchers would wish, and even be encouraged, to consider how research might impact on their professional lives and the organisations in which they work.

We do not intend, in our enthusiasm for the topic, to overclaim the benefits that a research perspective on workplace problem solving might bring. Nevertheless there are certain key features that a research framework and considered use of well-proven methods for gathering and analysing data can add to practitioners' enquiries. At the same time, these features act as criteria for high-standard reports or dissertations. They are:

- the situation of the problem within current contexts of knowledge base and policy and political frameworks,
- a clarification of the real issues,
- the use of the best evidence available,

- analysis which goes beyond description,
- interpretations which relate the here and now to past and future.

At first reading, these may appear quite modest claims, but we hope that as we elaborate them in this and later chapters this modesty will be revealed as false. Our moderation is enhanced by what we have not claimed for a research perspective on practitioner problem solving. Constant objectivity is the most obvious omission and will be discussed later. Similarly we have not proposed that research will find *the* answer. The variety of approaches to research that we shall be discussing do not allow such a wide-reaching assertion.

Taking a research perspective therefore means being orderly, considered, scholarly and scientific when setting your research agenda. This agenda will include selecting a question, designing the research study, choosing data-gathering techniques and deciding on appropriate methods of analysis and interpretation. A research perspective encourages attention to the appropriateness of data-collection methods and the soundness of the information gathered. It attempts, above all, to keep a focused yet responsive route in the quest for greater understanding of the issues under scrutiny. An orderly, considered and scientific emphasis is the key to gathering the sound information that is essential if decisions on practice are to be made on the basis of practitioner research.

So in answer, in part, to the question 'why do research?' our reply is that changes in practice need to be justified, monitored and often adjusted. Modifications consequently have to be based on evidence. By taking a research perspective we can at least feel that we have tackled the issues in a rigorous way. The other part of our answer takes us to what can be gained by practitioners who engage with existing research as part of the research process. Practitioner researchers are unlikely to have the time to make ground-breaking discoveries but they are likely to gain a great deal personally from becoming acquainted with work that has already been undertaken and from considering its relevance for their practice (see Edwards in press a and b for discussions of how engagement in research enhances professional practice). Evidence-based practice is becoming increasingly important in education, health, social work and related fields. The evidence base for practice in these fields is already enormous. Practitioner research which builds on these bases is one way of ensuring both more informed practice, and the continuing development of the relevant knowledge bases as practitioners add to them. The development of practice and of the knowledge bases that inform it can be very rewarding, but it can also provide its own tensions. This is particularly so if colleagues are not sharing the insights that research can offer. Researcher motivation is therefore an important concern. With that in mind we turn to the first and fundamental rule of practitioner research survival.

Be selfish

Being selfish is something few adults would, openly at least, admit to. Yet it is central to the sanity of the hard-pressed researcher. At the start of your project you are about to take on a considerable commitment which is probably in addition to many continuing demands on your time. We talk of 'your project' and 'your time' with reason, as in order to get the most out of a research project you will need to make personal investments of time and single-mindedness. The last thing you should want to happen is that you become bored or disenchanted with the study. Consequently it is sensible to ensure that the research project is focused around something that interests you and is not imposed by others.

But initial interest alone is not enough. The issues may turn out to be less gripping than you thought, or your own situation or professional interests may change. It is therefore important that you choose your topic and title with an eye to your own career development. Your study will probably be one stage in your developing professional expertise. It is perhaps wise to expend the energy to be invested in the project in propelling yourself in the direction you would wish to take. If all other motivation then fails you at least have the 'means to an end' pull of your own career development to encourage your completion.

Most people become so engrossed in their projects that motivation does not appear a problem. Usually over-motivation is closer to reality as family and friends have to take second place to the new obsession. But when motivation is lost it may be due to lack of selfishness or investment of self in the study at the outset.

So be selfish, focus on what interests you, think about your curriculum vitae and your future professional development as well as the impact your study might have on the workplace, and then step forward with confidence.

Personal support

The researcher, however selfish, need never be entirely isolated in his or her endeavours. Of course you will have the opportunity to demonstrate initiative, problem-solving, perseverance and even perhaps creativity, all of which are individual qualities. In addition you should also make sure that you have people with whom you can discuss your developing ideas. We will be examining the critical friend relationship in action research in Chapter 4. At this point we want to encourage you to join research discussion or seminar groups. Any opportunity to clarify your own ideas in discussion with others can only be advantageous to your own understanding and you should seize any chance to exercise your current research preoccupations. The availability of local discussion groups will vary, but your supervisor may be able to put you in touch with national networks and to recommend newsletters and conferences which match your own interests.

But of all the relationships you form while engaged in your project, that with your supervisor should have the potential to be the most useful. Its ultimate effectiveness lies more in your hands than in his or hers. Supervisors are busy people with many other concerns, and consequently the selfish researcher may find it necessary to assert his or her right to supervisor time and advice. Demand it! By and large the support you will receive from your supervisor will be in direct proportion to the amount you request. Do not try to be independent or be diffident about bothering him or her. Supervisors are professionals with valuable advice to give. You will save a lot of your time if you seek and use that advice.

Having arranged your tutorial sessions use them well. Write your own agenda and work through it. Let your tutor know if you don't understand any jargonistic shorthand, aim always at feeling clearer about your project and next actions. Don't leave the tutorial if you are still confused. If possible also arrange an e-mail link with your supervisor. But remember that supervisors do sometimes need time to reply. The message is that your supervisor is there to be used as a resource for you, so use the resource.

Keeping a research diary

Many supervisors encourage the use of a research diary. It can become the most important prop in the research process if you use it well. We would urge you to do that. We shall be looking at the more extensive reflective diaries used in action research in Chapter 4. Some researchers engaged in other forms of research also find reflective diaries of the kind outlined under data collection methods in Chapter 4 of considerable use. It may, therefore, be wise to read that section after reading this one if the idea has strong appeal.

An effective format for a research diary is a small, probably hard covered, notebook. Working from the front of the book you can note ideas and observations as they occur to you. We have warned you about obsessionality! Included in these notes might be ideas developed during case conferences or conversations with clients and colleagues, issues raised by reading reports, or thoughts that occur while looking at what is going on in your workplace. The diary might include your reactions to these ideas and so provide a record of the focusing process of deciding upon and developing a research topic. Working from the back of the notebook you can keep other factual information. This might include reference details of reports summarised in the press, articles suggested by colleagues, quotations and sources that seem useful, dates of important meetings. Indeed it might encompass any kind of factual information that could disappear from the mind of the over-stretched practitioner researcher.

The advantage of a diary is twofold. First, it can provide a legitimate source of data which can be drawn upon when addressing issues of design and methodology. It may be, for example, appropriate to explain and illustrate the evolution of the project from its inception. Second, it acts as a source of information in a way that is far more reliable than the memories of most practitioner researchers. Our advice is, therefore, if you are not already keeping a diary start now.

Choosing the question

One of the first tests of your relationship with your research supervisor is the selection of your research topic. You will, no doubt, have a general idea of the topic, and may even have been given some specific issues to tackle by your employers or colleagues. But this is only the first stage of the process. Above all your study needs to be manageable, which in most circumstances means that it can be carried out by one person, in the time

Figure 1.1 Defining the title

available. Consequently most research ideas have to undergo some rigorous fine tuning.

The most important element in Figure 1.1 is the research question. Get that right and the rest of the study should flow smoothly. As a result the choice of final question is not entirely directed by your burning interest. It is also driven by the implications of the appropriate research design, data collection method and system of analysis, as these place constraints on what might be feasibly completed by one researcher in the time available. For this reason alone it is a good idea to discuss your study, as soon as possible, with a supervisor or experienced researcher. In that discussion you will have to be mindful of two quite different perspectives on research that are available to the practitioner researcher.

A fundamental question

Consideration of the relationship between your research question and the design of your study (see Figure 1.2) leads you to the need to confront and answer the question which is at the root of the research process. The question is an apparently simple one.

Do you want to test out an idea which is drawn from existing theory and examine its ultimate impact on practice, or do you want to look at what is going on and try to make sense of that by teasing out themes and patterns and even in a small way begin to develop or question existing explanations? In research terms you are deciding whether you are taking a deductive (theory-driven) or inductive (data-driven) approach. Though, as you will discover, the relationship between theory and data is not quite as simple in either approach as we've suggested here.

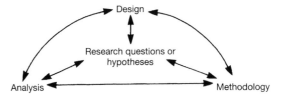

Figure 1.2 Relating the question to design and methodology

Two quite distinct models of science lie behind these alternatives. The deductive stance arguably draws upon a model of science derived from Newtonian mechanistic physics in which a simple linear connection between cause and effect can be discerned with relative ease. It also places great emphasis on the importance of clear evidence and the verification and falsification of propositions. Proponents of this view are sometimes described as logical positivists. The deductive-positivist starting point implies the use of control groups and matched samples and the manipulation of variables, of which much more in Chapter 3. It is a popular model, particularly with those who want clear information in a reasonably short period of time on which to, for example, base their resource allocation.

If we take an examination and evaluation of a reading improvement programme involving parents in working with their children at home as an example, we can begin to see the implications of this approach. A deductive model of evaluation would require that the children receiving parental support should be regarded as an experimental or treatment sample. They would be matched on reading age with children in a control sample. The experimental group would undergo the special programme while the children in the control group continue their normal practices. The reading ages of both groups would be assessed at the end of the programme and the differences between the scores of the two groups would be statistically tested to discover whether there was a significant difference between the groups.

Where, of course, there is a place for this kind of study it can be problematic when applied to the real-life situation described. Did perhaps the teachers of the treatment group spend less time on reading with the children knowing that the parents were doing more? What about the additional reading tuition children get from involvement in out-of-school activities? What was it about the reading programme that made the differences: the extra parental attention or the mechanics of the programme? What was the impact of the programme on other elements of classroom life? Clearly, controlling variables in real situations is very difficult for the practitioner researcher even, in some contexts, raising quite important ethical issues of entitlement.

The inductive alternative is not a simple solution. It too can draw on a model of physics. This time it is elements of post-Einstein physics which, in its discussion of waves and particles, allows us to see that there are different ways of seeing the same phenomenon, and in its explanations of the shifting complexity of matter helps us to see that linear cause and effect is an over-simplification and that any addition to a field of matter has some impact on that field. The last point provides an important warning to the researcher of the effects of his or her presence in the field of study. Consequently this approach has as its starting point a recognition of the complexity of the situations under scrutiny and the difficulty in teasing out the variables to be controlled and the patterns of cause and effect.

An inductive approach to the reading example we have been following would be to start by looking at what goes on between children and parents while they engage in the programme. It would then demand examination of what happens between the same children and their teachers when at school and working in the area of reading. A categorisation of patterns of behaviour could consequently be built up through content analysis of the data gathered. The status of these patterns would depend upon their frequency of occurrence and their appearance in other groups of people engaged in the same activity. Here we are beginning to describe an approach to theory building known as grounded theory, in which explanations of events are developed from detailed analysis of those events. The key feature of this approach is that explanations are driven to a great extent by data or phenomena rather than the imposition and narrow testing of a developed theory often from another context.

This simple explanation of inductive work is not meant to imply that the researcher enters the field devoid of theory: that would be impossible. Rather it indicates a tentativeness of theory and an openness to the effects of observable data. The particular approach has consequently been an attractive one for researchers who feel that existing theory may hold a sterile grip on the way that events are understood and interpreted. Much early feminist research, for example, had a great deal in common with the inductive framework just outlined.

The importance of personal theories, briefly alluded to in the previous paragraph, raises an important point. It is all too easy to adopt a simple distinction between deductive and inductive models by heralding the former as objective and the latter as subjective, and worse still by labelling one as quantitative and the other as qualitative research.

The issue of subjectivity is a complex one and needs to be addressed both in deductive and inductive approaches, as both demand rigour from the researcher as she or he tries to get a grip on reality. Again more of this in Chapter 3. As you will see later, qualitative data can, and often should, be rendered quantitative if grounded theory is your aim. Also some of the possible research designs we will be suggesting do not fit clearly in a distinctive category. Survey research, for example, aims at finding out what is going on, but is essentially quantitative.

Survey research also can be used deductively in 'before and after' studies or inductively in studies aiming at an initial examination of the field prior to further research. To further emphasise the weakness of over-simple categories of research, action research can aim at testing theory, but is as much concerned with process as outcome and would not involve the use of control groups (see Chapter 4).

Our advice is, therefore, that you should decide whether you will be taking a deductive or inductive angle on the events you are examining and then remain sensitive to the blurring of boundaries between the two approaches. The ultimate solution is often to create a mixed design and include both perspectives. An example of this might be the inclusion of case studies in an experimental study. But this may be beyond the scope of some smaller studies.

The feasibility of the research study

With these distinctions in mind we return to the practicalities of feasibility and opportunity. In Figure 1.2 we showed the untidy relationship between the research question, design, methodology and analysis. In later chapters we will expand these ideas in detail, but at this point we would like to begin to consider, in outline, some of the options available to you and their implications for selecting a feasible research focus and question.

Design options

Much of the research you will have read will have drawn upon data from large samples and may even have included the use of control groups to enable the researcher to make direct comparisons between, for example, treatments or experiences using the deductive model we have just described. While, as we have already indicated, this is a sound way to undertake research, it may not prove to be the most feasible or the most useful to the single-handed practitioner researcher.

Alternatives to the straightforward deductive approach create a range of other design options. These alternatives should be considered at the stage at which you decide upon the research question. Much will depend upon what you want your study to achieve. If you are interested in finding out simple facts about people and their lives or the general attitudes held by groups of people, maybe in order to make some intervention to improve a service to them at a later date, then a survey is the obvious choice. A survey would require you to distribute questionnaires or an attitude scale and gather descriptive data. These information-gathering techniques often provide useful information but rarely lead to the opportunity for the researcher to exhibit, to any great extent, any skills of data analysis, though attitude scales do give much more scope for the demonstration of analytic competencies than do simple questionnaires. Surveys also play an important part in evaluation studies to gauge the effect of an experience or treatment by collecting data before and after the event.

If you wish to take a more overtly inductive approach and probe a little deeper into finding out what is going on now, to look at processes and the ways in which others are making sense of a situation or event, then a case study or a progressive focusing design may be appropriate. If survey research aims at width of information from a relatively large sample, but with relatively little depth of understanding of what is actually going on, the converse is true of case study research. Here the focus is relatively narrow. It could be a ward of patients, a class of children, a counselling group, a family, three neonates. The study gains its strength from the richness of data gathered on the small focus. Case study allows you to look at processes and interpretations and to dig below the surface of the taken-for-granted.

It may be most appropriate that you use both survey and illustrative case study in a mixed design. Advantages of the combination include allowing you to take case studies to examine processes at work in, for example, a 'before and after treatment' survey study. A third option is one that can frequently be used to follow on from survey or case study work. This model involves the monitoring and evaluation of initiatives or developments which are being undertaken by the researcher in the course of his or her work. We shall describe this as action research in Chapter 4. A major concern of action research is the examination of both the outcome and processes of developmental action within one context. Like simpler versions of case study research it has a narrow focus and leads to increased understanding of one context and the processes at work. It also has a positive impact on practitioner confidence and esteem. Its aim is considered change and for that reason alone it proves attractive to many practitioners.

As well as the aims of various approaches to research you need to be aware of their limitations. While a sufficiently large and carefully chosen sample may allow generalisation of the research findings from a survey to a wider population, this is not the aim of most case study or action research. It is possible to come to some more general conclusions from case study work by the comparative analysis of individual cases. And it is commonplace to engage in team action research. But in action research, the emphasis is on institutional and personal change, and generalisations about the effectiveness of action research methods are the most that can reasonably be allowed.

Data collection options

We have already hinted at some of these. Survey methods clearly call for questionnaires or attitude scales. The smaller samples used in case study work require methods that allow greater depth of probing and certainly demand that you use more than one method of collecting data about a situation or event. The methods most frequently used include interviews, observations and written information (see Chapter 5 for these and others). All these methods take time to use and often time to analyse, and this factor needs to be taken into account when deciding on the feasibility of your study. For example, a one-hour interview will take up to six hours to type and can be analysed infinitely.

Action research draws on similar methods to those used by case study. But the focus here is largely upon the impact of your observation on your own understanding and practice. Some degree of self-revelation is necessary as the notion of the reflective, learning practitioner is central to the design, data collection methods and ways of analysing information. We shall be suggesting in Chapter 4 that the reflective diary should be a key vehicle for data collection and analysis.

The major feasibility issue in action research is the time available for the duration of the study. If the aim of the study is to follow an initiative or development it is necessary to ensure that the submission date for the report or dissertation gives you sufficient time to see the events through to implementation, completion or appropriate evaluation point.

Access to the field of study

At this point we return to the constraints that might be placed on your project. Access to information should never be taken for granted. It needs to be checked before you embark. We know of many studies where vague promises have led to disappointment when informants had second thoughts about co-operating, or written information was ultimately revealed to be 'confidential'. You may discover that you have to request permission from several layers of organisational hierarchy to ensure that access is available to you. It is therefore helpful to have ready a brief research protocol in which you outline, in lay terms, the purpose of the study, its design and the data collection methods to be used, what will be required of those who provide information, how the data will be presented (for example, using comments without referring to names, individual responses anonymised as numerical data in tables etc.) and who will see the final report. The protocol can then be discussed with the relevant gate-keepers. You may want to get written consent from the people you are to collect information from and may therefore decide to include a consent form as part of the brief protocol you give them. This strategy is often used, for example, when asking parents' permission to observe or interview their children. Consent forms usually indicate that the informant understands the nature of the research, and are signed by the researcher and by the informant or guardian.

It is important that you check that you will have access to all the respondents you need at the outset of the study, as an unwillingness to be involved may require changes in the design of the study. When undertaking research in health care settings it may also be necessary to gain the approval of the local ethics committee before starting the research. The approval process can take time and therefore needs to be started as soon as possible.

Once you are allowed access to the field you then have considerable responsibility as a researcher to the people whose worlds you are investigating and into whose lives you are intruding. This is particularly so when you are gathering information from people who have limited social power. These include, of course, children and clients of a service, but may also include junior or similar status colleagues. One of the challenges of social research is the need to keep a professional distance while dealing sympathetically with the feelings and interpretations of events revealed to you by respondents. Campaigning or 'passionate' research certainly has an important contribution to make to improving our social worlds but, we would argue, is something to be undertaken once the complexities of rigorous social research have been mastered.

Confidentiality is a key issue when working in the field. It applies not only to how data are presented but also to how researchers operate in the field as they move between groups of informants. We are now moving to the closely related issue of research ethics.

Research ethics

We suggest thinking about the ethics of a research project in the very early stages of planning the study. Most professional groups have codes of ethical behaviour which will underpin how members of those professions operate as researchers. The British Educational Research Association (BERA) has produced ethical guidelines which provide a useful framework and which is available on the BERA website. Its guidelines are based on the principle of responsibility to, in turn, the research profession, participants, the public and funders. The guidelines also address the researchers' right to publish and the limitations on this, intellectual ownership and relationships with employers. University research committees also often issue ethical guidelines and you may find that these meet your needs as an individual researcher. We do, however, suggest that you discuss ethical issues with your supervisor if you have one.

Responsibility to participants and to colleagues is usually the primary concern of practitioner researchers. These responsibilities require careful consideration and everyone engaged in a project needs to be aware of the implications of ethical responsibility. We therefore need to make sure that everyone discusses ethics and that guidelines are not simply given out to be filed away. When working with groups of practitioners, we allocate a couple of hours at the planning stage of a project or initiative for the production of a set of ethical guidelines for the particular project. We organise our discussion under the headings of:

- responsibility to participants,
- responsibility to colleagues,
- responsibility to funders,
- responsibility to ourselves.

After initial brainstorming under these headings we produce our own agreed code of behaviour. Examples of questions that might arise during a brainstorm are as follows, though not all projects raise all these questions.

- Will the data collection method cause pain or distress to participants?
- Am I satisfied that any conclusions reached are appropriately supported by enough evidence?
- Can I keep promises of confidentiality?
- Am I being sufficiently sensitive to cultural differences?
- Am I taking undue advantage of my position to gain information (e.g. from teachers in the school in which you are headteacher)?
- Does the research raise false hopes amongst the participants?
- Can I reproduce my findings in ways that authentically represent the concerns of participants?
- How can I present the data in a way that does not harm the respondents?

Responses to these questions may lead to statements in the agreed code of behaviour such as

- Individual respondents will not be named in the research report.
- Participants will be given a copy of the research protocol explaining their contribution, the time demands to be made on them and how the research will be reported.

- Any discussion of individual cases will remain confidential to the research team.

We clearly suggest that attention to ethical research, like attention to access to the field of study, is planned into the research process at the outset. A concern with the ethics of research may have considerable implications for research design.

Return to the question

Having taken many of these considerations into account you should be ready to start to focus down onto your research question(s). Figure 1.3 outlines the relationship between examples of the type of question you might wish to ask and the research design you might employ. You may wish to phrase your research question in a way that maintains its exploratory nature. Indeed it is argued (Taylor, 1977) that the aim of research should simply be to enable the researcher to ask a better question next time. Or you may wish to turn your question into an experiment requiring a hypothesis and then a null hypothesis ready for ultimate disproof (see Chapter 3). Whichever way you choose to proceed you will need to remain focused on your research questions throughout your study as you explore related literature, design or choose your data collection methods and present and discuss your findings.

★	
Type of question	Design
Is x different from y?	Experimental design requiring numerical data.
What is going on here?	Inferential design using case study and possibly progressive focusing. It may require both qualitative and numerical data.
How well does z work for me and my colleagues?	Action research with close attention to detail and context.
Did that intervention change practices?	Evaluation study using survey methods which may include questionnaires and observations. It will require mainly numerical data though qualitative data can be incorporated.

Figure 1.3 The relationship between design and question

Choosing a title

A useful way to start on this is to brainstorm the elements you wish to cover in your research question. If, for example, you want to examine the relationship between a staff development programme on time management and changes in the work habits of community nurses operating out of three general practices your brainstorm might look like Figure 1.4.

You will see that the brainstorm itself raises issues you might want to consider. Do you, for example, want to look at the processes by which the training is allowed to impact or do you want a simple outcome measure?

The next stage is to select the words from the brainstorm that best indicate the issues you expect the study to be addressing. It is useful at this point to think about the key words that might be used if your study were to be placed on a library database and accessed by other researchers. The words selected from Figure 1.4 might be:

community nurses   case study   staff development

comparative   time management   impact

These words could then produce the following title:

The impact of staff development in time management on the work of community nurses: a comparative case study.

A colon is often a useful device as it allows you to pull quite disparate elements of the brainstorm together.

Finally, check that the title really does reflect the research question you have set and that the creativity of the brainstorm has not led you astray and away from your original intentions.

staff development,   processes,

time management,

impact,

community nurses,

exploration,

case study,   three practices,

comparison

Figure 1.4 A title brainstorm

The structure of a written project

We shall be looking at all the conventions associated with presenting a written report in Chapter 7. Nevertheless it is important that you are aware of what is expected of you as you embark on the study, so that you can undertake your own time management. A very basic structure looks something like Figure 1.5. The percentages shown don't add up to 100 and are *indicative* of the proportion of total words to be used in each element. Different types of studies will require different structures and emphases. For example, it may be impossible to separate methodology, results and discussion in an action research study. This would mean that the final chapter becomes a much shorter discussion of implications following several chapters that may be separated by *phase of study* rather than the headings shown in Figure 1.5. Some research studies demand a process of successive focusing on events. Again the stark outline provided here would not be entirely appropriate.

Similarly, some studies may demand a very heavy literature review and others may have methodological innovation as a key point and require an emphasis there. We have given the basic outline as it stands because it captures the issues to be addressed somewhere within the final report and indicates what a logical order *might be*. Most researchers move a long way from this structure in their final presentations, and rightly so. But it is always useful to know what one version of the rules looks like as you start to plan. Our advice is that you at least glance at the options given in more detail in Chapter 7 before you begin to read around and plan your study.

Abstract Table of Contents		Approximate proportions
Chapter 1	Introduction	10%
Chapter 2	Review of Literature	25%
Chapter 3	Design of Research	10%
Chapter 4	Discussion of Methodology	15%
Chapter 5	Presentation of Results	10%
Chapter 6	Discussion of Results	25%
Appendix		
References		

Figure 1.5 A basic dissertation structure

Ready to start

Clearly there are a lot of decisions to make before you commit yourself to a particular route on this quest for greater understanding. The decision making cannot be rushed as the right choices help to ensure, but don't totally guarantee, that your time will not be wasted by backtracking or restarting. Having committed yourself to a particular direction you need to endeavour to become aware of all the implications and check that your study is feasible. Having done that, it is time to beg the tolerance of family and friends and, with research diary in hand, start to pick your way along the path with all the attention to detail that such a journey demands.

Further reading

Martyn Hammersley's critique of the misguided distinction between qualitative and quantitative research is essential reading for anyone concerned with some of the conceptual issues which underpin the process of research: Hammersley, M. (1992) *What's wrong with ethnography?*, Routledge.

Bickman, L. and Rog, D. (eds) (1998) *Handbook of applied social research methods*, Sage, is a useful collection of papers each tackling a major issue in the practice of social research. It includes, for example, chapters on research ethics, research design, qualitative research and quasi-experimentation.

If your research interest is practice and its development you may enjoy Seth Chaiklin's discussion of the relationship between research and practice in a chapter which concludes a collection of papers on the topic of understanding practice in context within an activity theory framework. Chaiklin, S. (1993) 'Understanding the social scientific practice of understanding practice', in S. Chaiklin and J. Lave (eds) *Understanding practice: perspectives on activity and context*, Cambridge University Press.

For health and nursing research there is a fast growing range of literature. These include Clifford, C. (1997) *Nursing and health care research: a skills-based introduction*, Prentice-Hall; Reed, J. and Proctor, S. (eds) (1995) *Practitioner research in health care*, Chapman and Hall; Burnard, P. and Morrison, P. (1994) *Nursing research in action: Developing basic skills*, Macmillan; and McGee, P. and Notter, J. (1995) *Research appreciation: an initial guide for nurses and health care professionals*, Quay Books.

Chapter 2

Making notes and using a library

This chapter concentrates upon aspects of study skills that will be important to you as a busy researcher. Time is limited, and it is necessary to consider how best to use it. Early attention to the taking of notes and how to use supporting literature will save you time at a later stage. Some of these points may appear self-evident, but the experience of many practitioners has shown that there can be hiccups in the best set of notes, or the most thorough literature search. As you start your research quest you need to be clear about the kind of text-based information you will need to acquire and store.

Types of information

Having decided on the research question and the title, you are now ready to think about the different types of information you will need. These will have different sources and demand different skills from you as you seek and use them.

- *Library-based information.* This will include articles, reports and books which will be used to support your arguments as you review the literature available and your decisions as you select your research design and research methods.
- *Local information.* This may include material produced by the group or institution you are examining, for example, local evaluation reports or general information for patients. It will also include background details on the setting of your study, for example, the average number of patients seen in one day or the range of disabilities treated.

- *Research data.* Some local material may well become data which can be carefully analysed along with other written texts. The bulk of your research data will, however, be collected using the methods we discuss in Chapters 4 and 5.

In this chapter we shall be concentrating on the search for and use of library-based material. But we would urge you to be open-minded about the importance of what we describe as local information. Be prepared to consult a range of documents. A set of papers or minutes may carry as much weight as an article in a learned journal.

If we take as an example an evaluation study of a changing school or health care setting, the following fields of literature and information would need to be searched.

- Key concepts in evaluation in the public sector.
- Methodologies employed in public sector evaluation.
- Local information including previous evaluations and relevant background information.

The university library network will help with literature in key concepts and methodologies. Local information will require more ingenious enquiry, but could be supported by library-based information retrieval systems, one of which, the UK National Online Management Information System, will be described later in this chapter.

Finally, but not least, you will be given a few hints about using the Internet.

Use of the library

To search effectively you will need to define your subject(s) clearly in order to know what subject headings to search, what sort of material you want, over what period you require information and what sources you are going to use. General advice would be to favour recent articles. Internal and external examiners give credit to contemporary literature and cross-referencing. Some subjects may have a long historical background, but the early literature on the topic should not be allowed to remove the main focus of interest away from recent publications.

To support new readers at libraries, some library staff have set up short interactive induction programmes. As cataloguing systems may vary, familiarity with one system does not mean you will be at home in every library you visit. The use of exercises contained within induction programmes helps stimulate reference to a cross-section of books and literature and will give you a good start. But remember that librarians are trained to support you in your search for information. So do use their expertise whenever you need help.

Periodicals provide a considerable amount of information, including original papers, reports of completed and ongoing research and conference proceedings. Published at regular frequent intervals, periodicals are able to supply information which is more up-to-date than that found in most books. Books, however, can offer more detail than is possible in an article. Theses will yield a wealth of information. The bibliographies or reference listings of all of these publications are often invaluable sources of additional reading. Research studies may also include useful appendices or tables. Government circulars and reports (e.g. those produced by the Department for Education, or by the Department of Health) generally have a limited circulation initially and can be difficult to trace. Some specialist libraries may have them; otherwise, you may need to use an inter-library loan facility. Some local government reports may be available in libraries, but usually they have to be supplied by the local authority itself. A letter to the relevant department is often successful.

The material you require may be available on the shelves of your library. Where books are not within the bookstock of your library, then inter-library loan facilities normally exist. Sometimes there may be a small charge for their use. Many UK libraries will have a facility to enable you to examine a database on CD-ROM, *Boston Spa Books*, which gives details of the 500,000 books in the British Library's national inter-library loan collection (another database, *Bookbank*, also provides details of books published in Britain). *Books in Print* (UK and USA) allows you to identify all books that have been published and are currently in print. Equivalent systems operate in most other countries.

It is possible that you may be able to consult a number of libraries in your locality in order to undertake your literature search. The inter-library loan facility may operate on a reciprocal basis between a number of regional or local libraries. Alternatively, the British Library at Boston Spa in Yorkshire operates a service for books and for periodical articles. You should enquire at your library for the local arrangements to assist you in your search. British researchers in the north of England may find it of value to visit the British Library Centre at Boston Spa; photocopies can be made there, but they appreciate prior warning of your visit. The address is Thorpe Park Trading Estate, Boston Spa, Wetherby, West Yorkshire, LS23 7BQ (phone 01937 546000).

Using indexing and abstracting services

Another source of information is provided by published index and abstract compilations. In the UK, theses may be traced through the *Index to Theses* which gives details, including abstracts, of theses accepted for higher degrees by British Universities. Another publication, *Dissertation Abstracts*, includes American material. Again, similar systems operate in countries other than Britain. Most academic libraries keep up-to-date versions of these publications.

Other indexing services list all the material published in specified periodicals and are produced monthly, bimonthly or quarterly, with annual cumulations. They are arranged by subject heading and author and cite the author and title of the article and the title, volume, issue number, year of publication and pagination of the periodical. They do not give any more information on the content of the article; it is usually necessary to read the actual article to assess its relevance.

Abstracting services provide the same information and also a summary, or abstract, of the article which may supply enough detail for the researcher to know if it is relevant. We give the British systems as exemplars only.

The appropriate index or abstracting periodical depends upon your subject areas. Most social science, health, business or education research is likely to be multi-disciplinary. Articles on health education and physical education are included along with general education in the *British Education Index*, on community and women's studies in the *British Humanities Index* (which also includes the quality newspapers), on community health, medicine, psychology, psychiatry and social work in the *Social Sciences Index*, and on nursing and health in the *Applied Social Sciences Index and Abstracts* which includes summaries of articles. Research abstracts may be published by government departments; for example, the Department of Health publishes *Health Service Abstracts* (monthly) and *Nursing Abstracts* (quarterly with an annual cumulation). The former covers a broad range of subjects within the Health Service, whilst the latter covers completed ongoing research in the UK of relevance to nursing, midwifery and health visiting.

Searching retrospectively through annual cumulations can be very time-consuming. A rapidly increasing number of indexes and abstracts are now available as databases on compact disc. This enables you to search a vast amount of material very quickly and print out a selected list of references. Titles of such databases (together with a short note to indicate subject area) include the following:

- *ABI-Inform.* Business and management.
- *Aquatic Sciences and Fisheries.* Freshwater and marine environment.
- *Art Index.* Visual arts.
- *Bookbank.* British books in print.
- *Bookfind.* Range of British and US books.
- *Cinahl.* The Cumulative Index of Nursing and Allied Health Literature.
- *ERIC.* Education.
- *Index to Theses.* British and Irish theses.
- *INSPEC.* Engineering and science (Physics, Electrical and Electronic Engineering, Computers and Information Science).
- *Lexis.* Law/legal issues.
- *Life Sciences.* Biological and life sciences.
- *Medline.* A medical database.
- *PSYCLIT.* Psychological abstracts.
- *SCAD + CD.* EEC
- *UK Official Publications.* Parliamentary, non-parliamentary (HMSO, now called The Stationery Office) and non-HMSO publications.
- *Volnet.* Community development, voluntary action and social policy.

Many of these will be found in university and larger college libraries. Such libraries will have instruction sheets/material that will help you in the use of such databases. However, this list is by no means exhaustive and new databases are being produced at the present time. Again, a qualified librarian will be able to help if you are unsure about which you might use. In some cases, especially where you might be examining a topic in an inter-disciplinary area (e.g. management and a clinical setting), you might need to consult a number of such databases; for other researchers the task should be more straightforward.

Information retrieval systems

For some researchers the material being sought will be located within newspapers, national census reports or other statistical databases. Again, your college or university library will assist you in the location and use of any appropriate information retrieval system. Most universities, for example, will have access to a retrieval system for the National Census.

The example presented here is that of NOMIS (National Online Management Information System). It is a computerised employment information system developed at the University of Durham on behalf of the Department of Employment. In national use since 1982, NOMIS allows access to official statistics on employment, vacancies and population, together with facilities to compare and analyse data on a wide range of areas from local to national levels. The complete database contains information for the whole of Great Britain.

Whilst the use of NOMIS has been recognised by national and local authorities, it is also of much value to researchers. It is a ready means of obtaining the most recent, reliable and detailed data on employment and other material. Such information is available at a range of geographical levels, and some data analysis facilities are available within the system itself (graphs, percentages, etc.). Whilst not a total list of the data available on NOMIS, the following list illustrates the breadth of material.

(i)   Census of population data to ward level.
(ii) Census of employment total since 1971 – specifically employment by industrial classification for local travel-to-work areas.
(iii) Unemployment data for at least ten years at national level, and for at least six years at ward level.
      Unemployment totals for males and females are produced every month. Analyses by age and duration categories are produced every quarter.

(iv) Vacancy data for at least twelve years, both unfilled and filled.
(v) Annual population projections from 1981 to 2001.
(vi) National Health Service migration data sets.

Such data are available for many scales of study, including the following:

(a) Wards,
(b) Travel-to-work areas,
(c) Local authority districts,
(d) Parliamentary constituencies,
(e) Regions.

Reading existing research

When you are reading relevant articles, journals, books and papers, you will need to ask yourself a series of important questions:

- Am I selecting the right kind of material?
- Am I achieving a cross-section or balance of material on this topic?
- How much should I read?
- How should I analyse this material?

Am I selecting the right kind of material?

There is no easy answer to this; it is often a question of judgement. Using key words when, for example, searching through an abstracting system may provide large numbers of articles and other material. However, until you examine them you may not know whether they are appropriate. Just because an article has been located does not make it relevant! Do not therefore order each item that a search has produced. Take the list to your tutor and discuss it. Or start by ordering the most obviously relevant and recent studies. Articles and books that are available in your library can be quickly skimmed before reading. Most articles have brief abstracts. The relevance of any book can be gauged by looking for key words in the book's index. And remember, books do not need to be read from cover to cover. Be selective.

Am I achieving a cross-section or balance of material on this topic?

Again there is no straightforward answer. When there is a lot of available material in your research field, you need to take care to achieve a balance of different viewpoints. Sometimes the areas of debate can be gleaned from standard texts or articles that might review ongoing research. Be guided by your tutor. Try to avoid large numbers of reports by the same author. This might help to provide balance. In many health care fields, there are few applications of some topics, for example counselling, to specific professions. In these situations, don't be parochial; look at what other health care professionals are writing about that topic.

How much should I read?

This may be limited by the amount of available literature. Alternatively, it might be constrained by the time that you have allowed yourself in order to collect information for your research report. Rarely is there an expected number of references for research projects. Clearly, to present a report citing just five books or articles will be frowned upon. Likewise, there is little justification in presenting a bibliography with 100 citations for a 4,000-word report. Whilst 20 or 40 different items may be appropriate, these figures are indicative rather than prescriptive. Above all you need to demonstrate that you are aware of key current issues in your field of study and are familiar with the literature.

How should I analyse this material?

Critical questions that deserve attention are as follows:

(a)   What have I learned from this work? Does it tell me anything new? Is there any descriptive information that may be useful for my own study?

(b)   To whom are the findings addressed? Research is often undertaken and/or written up for a particular audience; does this impinge upon my own study?

(c)   To what extent is this piece of research a product of its time and place? Does it reflect a set of preoccupations which are not now entirely relevant? Would we ask the same questions now? If not, why not?

(d) What conclusions are made in the work? Are they generalisable, or is the setting such that the conclusions made may not be replicable? Are there particular factors that are of value which can be identified in my own study? Can the design and methodology be replicated in my own work?

(e) Does this research replicate an earlier study? Will my own research fit into a sequence of research studies?

(f) What model of research does this article fit? To what extent is the setting real or artificial? Might a different research design have produced different results/ conclusions?

(g) Is there anything missing? Does the earlier research present me with an opportunity to undertake new work under similar conditions?

(h) Has the research presented me with suggestions for further research, or with warnings about the type of research that I have in mind?

(i) How does this author's treatment of the key theme differ from that of another author? What might be the reasons? Answers may be found in the different starting points, concerns, or contexts of the different authors.

Making notes and storing information

You need to store information on what you read for two purposes. The first is to give you quick access to the source of an idea or argument. The second is to inform the writing-up process. Two systems of note-taking and storage are therefore required. But they are closely inter-related.

Brief records

Keeping a card box file system in which you briefly record everything you have read or skimmed is an essential activity. It will prove to be additionally valuable as you come to complete the bibliography required when you present your report or dissertation. The same information can be kept on a personal computer. As well as being a record of a text that has been read, the card should contain some notes or key words which may at a later date invite a return to the full text or the longer notes you have made.

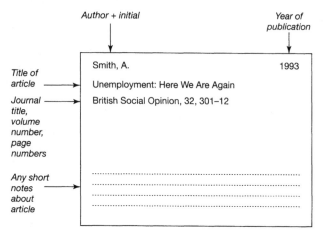

Figure 2.1 Index card

An example of the type of information that should be contained on an index card is shown in Figure 2.1.

On your card (or computer) index of what you have read, you should include the following information:

- *Books*
  - Author's surname and initials
  - Date of publication
  - Title in full (and any subtitle)
  - Edition (if not the first)
  - Publisher's name and place of publication
- *Periodicals* (in addition to author, date and title – as above)
  - No of volume(s)
  - No(s) of pages

These index cards should be cross-referenced to any notes you may have taken as you read the text that is shown on the card.

Extensive notes

We have already indicated the sort of questions you might be asking as you read the material available. But unless your memory is photographic you will probably find that note-taking will help you to get a purchase on what is being argued in the text.

If one purpose of note-taking is to increase your understanding of what you are reading, blind copying from the text is a waste of time. It is also dangerous, as you may unwittingly reproduce the original text as your own words, be accused of plagiarism, and probably be failed if your dissertation or report contributes to your course work. It is, however, often useful to be able to quote the telling phrase or even lengthy extract from a text. If you do you *must* acknowledge the origin. To help you to do this you should note the page numbers in the original text as you copy out the quotations. You will require them when you write up. You should also indicate, with quotation marks, that the words are taken directly from the text.

It is also useful to keep wide margins when you take notes so that you can write in additional comments and cross-references to other texts when you reread them.

You will develop your own style of note-taking. But you will begin to see that the author's key ideas are often evident in sub-headings and in key paragraphs. You will learn to distinguish between assertion or suggestion and evidence. Also you will discover that much can be gained from reading the beginnings and endings of articles and books. The corroborative detail of the main body of the text may not be essential for your purposes – though that is not the case with this text!

Your notes will need an indexing system. This can simply be a sheet of paper (contents page) in the front of your note file which lists notes by author of text and by topic and indicates in which section of your file it can be found.

The great value of keeping your notes and data in good order lies in the information retrieval process. The hard-pressed researcher does not wish to waste valuable time chasing up information collected some weeks or months earlier. By keeping good records, you can find material again if necessary. In addition, the task of referencing material in the text and compiling your list of references and bibliography becomes more bearable.

Use of the Internet

You will find other books (e.g. Winship and McNab, 1996) that have comprehensive guidance about use of the Internet. Via a personal computer at home, at work or at your university library, you can gain ready access to large amounts of information.

You can use the Internet to browse documents via the World Wide Web. A form of library searching is possible through accessing different subject headings. In most cases these are being updated on a regular basis, thus allowing you to gain information quickly about authors, topics, articles and books. Journals and publications are being published electronically in ever-growing numbers. However, because of this information explosion, there is a need for you to structure your search queries, and to develop search strategies to help you access good quality information sources.

Summary

Many of the points we have discussed may appear obvious. However, the key point of this chapter has been to ask the hard-pressed researcher to take great care in this part of the research process, and to suggest a degree of organisation over what otherwise can turn into a forest of paper, photocopies and paper cuttings.

When undertaking the note-taking, literature search and reading of other research, remember three things:

- Keep the research question in your mind at all times. You will discover many interesting ideas. Some may be intellectual cul-de-sacs. Other ideas may be thought-provoking and will enable you to analyse your own situation in a new light. Make sure, however, that you can see the implications and links with the aims and objectives of your own work.

- The scale of library work and note-taking will depend upon the research question, the time-scale available, and the nature of the project. The researcher utilising action research or grounded theory as the basis for a research project will find the task rather different to somebody setting up an experimental research project. The former researchers will need to be constantly returning to available literature, the latter may be able to see the literature search as just one stage in the study.

- Be orderly. Much time can be saved by developing your own information retrieval system whereby, with some speed, you can access manually or through the use of a microcomputer the material that is relevant to your written report or dissertation.

Further reading

Berger, R.M. and Patchener, M.A. (1988) *Planning for research: a guide for the helping professions*, Sage. This is a useful handbook, including sections on literature searching and use of abstracts, especially for those in the caring professions and social sciences.

Hakin, C. (1982) *Secondary analysis in social research*, Allen & Unwin.

Hakin, C. (1987) *Research design: strategies and choices in the design of social research*, Allen & Unwin. Both of these books provide excellent guides for those contemplating secondary research and the use of administrative records.

Whittaker, K. (1972) *Using libraries: an informative guide for students and general users*, André Deutsch. Whilst dated, the text is a suitable general guide for those undertaking a piece of library research. More recent texts include the following:

King, E. (1987) *How to use a library: a guide for young people and students*, Northcote House.

Moore, N. (1987) *How to do research*, 2nd edn, Library Association.

Winship, I. and McNab, A. (1996) *The Student's Guide to the Internet*, Library Association. This is a good example of one of the current books that gives you an introduction to the use of the World Wide Web and Internet.

Chapter 3

Designing a study

Selecting the design

Having decided both upon the focus of your research and upon the title of your study, you will need to select the appropriate design for that research study. Adams and Shvaneveldt (1991) describe research design as a 'plan, blueprint or guide for data collection and interpretation – sets of rules that enable the investigator to conceptualise and observe the problem under study' (p. 103). We agree with this definition and emphasise that a well-designed study sets the researcher free to explore and find the connections that make research so interesting. The different research designs we are looking at in this chapter are sub-divided into four areas:

- survey research;
- experimental research;
- case studies;
- progressive focusing designs.

Conceptually there is some overlap between these designs; for example, both case studies and surveys are largely descriptive and exploratory. In addition, different designs can draw on similar research methods and forms of analysis. This chapter concentrates on those categories of design frequently used by researchers in the social sciences. Action research, which is also a valuable approach, is examined separately in Chapter 4.

Some research questions do not easily fit the typology of design we have presented, but much of value can be gained from consideration of the different issues that relate to each research design. At each stage of the research process it is essential to consider later implications of that process. For example, when designing your study, you will need to recognise the different methods that can or cannot be undertaken and the issues that arise in the analysis of data. Can the design, for example, generate enough data to allow the kind of analysis that you would wish? Figure 3.1 identifies the major research designs. In highlighting the major features of these procedures, certain key advantages are listed, together with some of the research foci covered by the relevant research design. Whilst Figure 3.1 is not exhaustive, it does serve to illustrate at a glance how/when such

Design	When used	Why
Survey	Snapshot of setting/ views/attitudes	Speed of gaining information.
	Identify relationships	Large amount of data can be gained with relatively little effort.
	Demographic and epidemiological research. *Patient/client/use satisfaction surveys.* *Market research* *Workload evaluation and human resource planning.* *Monitoring standards.*	
Experimental	Testing purposes	No other design can test for causation.
	To identify causation (e.g. effects of x upon y)	
	Laboratory-based research. Some psychological research. *Trialing of drugs, equipment, dressings; clinical assessment.*	
Case studies	In-depth study of individual/area/setting	Allows past and present study, and for chronology to be established. Allows interaction with context to be observed.
	Historical research; many evaluation studies. *Action research often starts with case studies.*	
Progressive focusing	Understanding behaviour and social settings	Permits 'natural' studies
		Feedback may be speedy since no artificial conditions may be required.
	Sociological research.	

Figure 3.1 Research design: characteristics of the four common designs

research designs might be used. The emphasis of this section is to assist you in selecting the 'best fit' design for your purpose.

Within this chapter, there will be some link between research design and appropriate research methods, together with examples of the type of project, and the advantages and limitations of each design. No single design fits all research questions and research situations. Rather, the hard-pressed researcher is presented with design scenarios from which to choose. It is hoped that these templates will assist you in making your choice.

Surveys and descriptive research

There are different types of descriptive research that may be worth considering. Each can provide useful information for researchers; here three key types of survey have been isolated for further attention.

Historical and documentary research

Many research questions rely upon the use of documentary sources at some stage in their design. In some cases this may relate to a historical document; for example, parish records, population statistics, the development of a hospital in the mid-Victorian period or of church schools in the nineteenth century. In other cases the documents are more recent and might relate to minutes of meetings, clinic attendance records, or of unpublished papers drawn up by a member of staff. The rationale for such research rests with the lack of any alternative. Limitations upon such work rest with the nature of the documentary evidence. Platt (1981) discusses the use of documents; some of the points are raised here:

- Availability of documents: you are limited to what you can get.
- The authenticity of documents: are they reliable and valid documents?
- Sampling: how far is this possible in the case of documentary evidence?
- The making of inferences, with difficulties of laying hands on supplementary information desirable to assist inference.

Platt concludes 'that there are important senses in which documentary research has problems which are not significantly different from those of research using other data sources' (p. 49). The use of documentary sources raises certain technical problems, but their value for the hard-pressed researcher should not be under-estimated.

Advantages of documentary research

• Specific to the context of the research.

• Often few other alternatives.

Disadvantages of documentary research

• Limited availability.

• Reliability and validity of documents.

• Sampling often not possible.

• Difficulties of making inferences.

Longitudinal studies

This is a form of developmental research where data are gathered over an extended period of time. A number of national studies have gained prominence where cohorts of people have been surveyed at regular periods of time (Wilkinson, 1986). For hard-pressed researchers, such research over a long time-scale is impossible; however, dissertations and some forms of independent study (especially on part-time degree or diploma programmes) do permit some research over a more limited period of time (e.g. a three-month period). These would be short-term longitudinal studies. For example, a representative sample of people could be selected, and then surveyed at regular intervals to examine changing attitudes over time with respect to an organisational change. Sometimes a mix of cross-sectional and longitudinal designs is possible; for example, you might be comparing groups of children from years 10, 11, 12 and 13 through a term or year in one comprehensive school. This allows a diary of activities to be compiled, the researcher to gather information at particular time intervals and at least get a sense of long-term differences by comparing cohorts. Some market research teams and opinion pollsters regularly use such techniques. For hard-pressed researchers the most obvious use of longitudinal survey design is in the before and after measures relating to a specific intervention.

Advantages of longitudinal research

• Examination of a group of individuals over time.

• No difficulties in establishing matching individuals at different points in time.

Disadvantages of longitudinal research

• Problems of retention of subjects (e.g., children in a school or households in the general population tend to move and there may be problems in retaining the sample for the whole study period).

• When individuals within the sample identify themselves as special in some way, there may be a tendency for them to act in a manner different from how they would normally (the 'Hawthorne Effect').

Cross-sectional studies

These can be undertaken at a variety of scales. At the macro-scale they include the decennial census organised by the Office for Population, Census and Surveys (OPCS), whilst at the micro-scale, these studies include attitude or opinion studies of staff working in an educational or health-care setting. The survey is a valuable tool for the researcher. Such studies are snapshots of the setting at a particular point in time. They are largely descriptive, highlighting what exists, but they can also form the basis for some statistical analyses (e.g. correlation studies), whereby the collection of data allows the researcher to seek relationships between data.

The scope of surveys varies. Their scale ranges from a national or international study to that of a local workplace setting. They can incorporate the findings of a few, or of a very large number of people. If you are going to use statistical analyses beyond those of descriptive statistics, you will need to recognise that a large sample will be required (a size of at least 30 is given in most textbooks).

Examples of survey design include the following examples from student projects:

(a) Effects of unemployment upon health. A comparison of 30 employed and 30 unemployed people. A questionnaire was distributed by hand to all 60 people.
(b) Influence of television viewing amongst seven-year-olds. This study begins with a questionnaire administered to a stratified sample of seven-year-olds.
(c) Standard setting in residential homes. This survey included checklists completed by managers in over 40 residential homes.

Issues in survey design

Chapter 5 examines research methods involved in survey research, but it is appropriate to identify a number of issues which relate to overall survey design:

- No survey is perfect; however, the aim of the research is to avoid error and bias as much as possible, and to proceed in a logical manner.
- A pilot study, gives the opportunity for a questionnaire or interview to be examined closely before the main survey is undertaken. The pilot study should not include people/ settings from the main study. The actual size of a pilot depends upon factors such as the purpose of the study and access to subjects. As an indicative figure, a pilot study should consist of approximately 10 per cent of the overall sample size.
- The sample of people or settings should be as representative as possible. There is an extensive literature on sampling, but for the hard-pressed researcher, the nature of the sample may be determined by the research question and the research setting. On occasions, the number of possible respondents may be so small as to make sampling an issue of little concern. In other circumstances,

you will utilise an opportunity sample; for example, children in a class, colleagues in a work setting, clients in your area. However, on other occasions you will need to consider how you will select your representative sample from a larger population. The sample of subjects should be as typical of the overall population as possible. We shall be examining sampling later in this chapter.

- Accessibility to your study group. You should consider whether this is likely to be a problem. Within health care settings, you may have to present a case to an ethics committee in order that patients can be interviewed as part of a research project. Within schools you may have to seek permission of senior management before undertaking a project involving parents, pupils, or staff. Many good ideas can be thwarted by lack of access to the appropriate people.

- Size of the survey. In some cases the number of 'subjects' is predetermined; for example, if you have 23 staff in a workplace setting and you wish to undertake a questionnaire survey, then there is little point in reducing the size of the survey. The main consideration for survey size is that of statistical analysis; there is no single rule. However, for some statistical tests, you will need at least 30 'subjects'. In addition, for some of these tests (e.g. chi-squared test) you will need to ensure that there are no fewer than five responses in any single category. Again, this points to larger, rather than smaller, sample sizes. So, if you are considering a survey that allows generalisation to a larger population, make sure that you are maximising those opportunities by undertaking a large enough survey.

- You should aim to have as large a response rate to your survey as possible. Again, there is no single criterion for those returns. However, a figure should be in excess of 60 per cent. A lower figure would raise questions about the appropriateness of the survey design, the representativeness of the sample or of the overall research process.

Planning a survey

When planning a survey there are a number of key stages that need to be considered. These are considered in Figure 3.2 (adapted from Davidson, 1970). In any survey you must emphasise

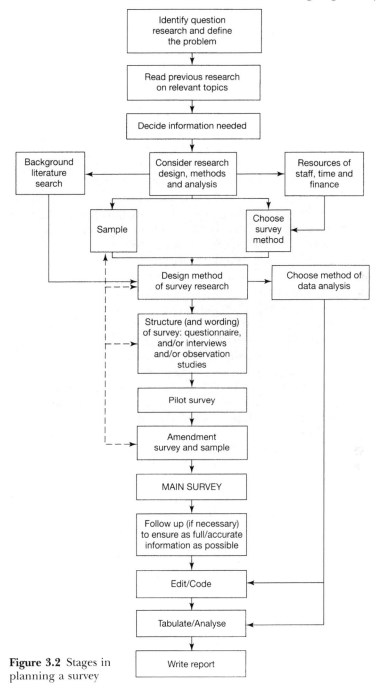

Figure 3.2 Stages in planning a survey

the importance of the research question, and how initial preparation is very important for subsequent stages of the survey.

You should consider different techniques of gathering information; a large number of surveys involve questionnaires, but interviews and observational studies may also form part of a survey. Difficulties in the use of questionnaires, through issues such as low response, have led some researchers to be disenchanted with their use.

In most cases survey designs involve collecting information from a sample of people or settings, rather than from the whole population. Different types of sample are possible:

- *Simple random sampling.* Each individual has an equal chance of being selected. The sample is selected at random from a list of the population (the sampling frame).
- *Systematic sampling.* Similar to above, but the sample is selected in a systematic fashion (e.g. every fifteenth person, every third child).
- *Stratified sampling.* The population (e.g. all twelve-year-olds in one school, all the health professionals in one health authority) is sub-divided into homogeneous groups, with each group having similar characteristics (e.g. sex, ability, previous primary school). In a survey of different health professionals, there would be a need to ensure an appropriate representation of each health profession. Sub-dividing the population into smaller groups (e.g. nurses or occupational therapists) makes this possible. The proportion of each professional group in the wider population should be reflected in the sample.
- *Cluster sampling.* This is appropriate for dispersed, geographical settings. As a refinement of stratified sampling it ensures a random sample of people in specific locations, rather than a small number of individuals in each setting over a large geographical area. For example, surveys of continuing education amongst nurses working in community settings might concentrate efforts in a small number of clinics and of teams of district nursing staff (e.g. psychiatric nurses) rather than across a large number of settings.
- *Snowball sampling.* In this form, you, the researcher, identify a small number of individuals with the characteristics that you require (e.g. teenage truants). The design is established

in such format that the initial sample provides you with information concerning others about whom you knew little at the start.

No set of guidelines or criteria exist to establish the most appropriate sampling type for all situations. However, the best advice is to seek as representative a sample as possible. For example, you may be designing a survey using an interview schedule with a cross-section of teachers, youth workers or nurses across an organisation. You would need to be satisfied that the sub-samples of staff you select at different grades, locations or with particular responsibilities represent the breakdown of staff in the organisation and that the interview schedule allows you to pick up on their different perspectives. This attention to representation would allow you to address any questions about bias or irrelevance in the sampling for your organisational survey. Do take care that you don't end up relying on an opportunity sample that fails to give you the wealth of information that you may wish to acquire.

Pilot studies are very important for survey design. They should be the preliminary step to the main study, mirroring the method, approach and questions. However, the pilot survey enables modifications to take place. As a result of pilot work changes could be made to the instructions, the sample, the question content, wording or sequence. In some cases pilots can assist decisions made about data analysis. Even if you are considering a postal questionnaire (please note that these are notorious for their low response rate) a pilot study should be administered personally in order to secure swift feedback from respondents. The pilot study might be the administration of six or ten questionnaires to staff working in a setting similar to that of the main survey, or the trial of an observation schedule in a classroom or clinic setting. This preliminary exercise allows a number of methodological difficulties to be resolved at an early stage and indicates your intention to be rigorous as you undertake your research.

Advantages of good survey work

- Provides a lot of information fairly speedily.

- Identifies some relationships between the data.

- Ensures confidentiality and anonymity of respondents when data are reported.

- Reliability is high, e.g. questionnaires can be used with different groups and over time.

- Speed of analysis (can be coded and edited quickly).

- The researcher retains 'control' over the research process.

- It is a valuable descriptive and exploratory design.

Disadvantages of survey work

- Produces a large volume of information (what do I do with it all?).

- Data collected may be superficial.

- Response rate to questionnaires may be poor and follow-up procedures are expensive and time-consuming.

- Little indication of causation and of factors affecting issues under scrutiny.

- Validity of material (it may be reliable, but is it valid?).
  Is it gathering information that really matters to the participants under scrutiny?

- Researcher bias and subjectivity in the methods adopted and interpretation of data (you are limited to the questions you feel are important).

Experimental research

This model is based on a scientific tradition which has been shaped for social science research. Described as the 'Traditional Deductive Model' or 'Hypothetico-deductive Model', it forms the mainstay of positivist research.

However, as already indicated in Chapter 1, it is not useful to see too clearly a distinction between deductive and inductive models of research. The inductive researcher who attends to the messages from a constant stream of information provided by the data gathered makes sense of the messages by tentatively applying theoretical frameworks to them. Similarly, as you can see in Figure 3.3, the research hypothesis used in the deductive research process outlined in the figure is in part at least derived

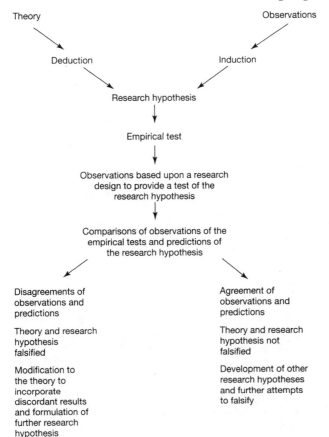

Figure 3.3 Experimental research design (adapted from Kiess and Bloomquist, (1985)

from careful observation of the research settings and is in that sense inductive.

The major distinguishing quality of positivist deductive research is the search for causality, with an expectation that variables, for example, age, sex, method of working, outcomes of projects, can be teased out, clearly identified and seen as separate and distinct items to be considered. In some cases this is unproblematic (e.g. age and sex); in others it is less easy.

Figure 3.3 outlines a typical experimental research design and indicates both its origin in current theoretical assumptions and careful observation, and the possible impact of empirical testing on the beliefs and actions of practitioners.

Experimental research is concerned primarily with the testing of a single factor upon two groups/situations. This single factor ('independent variable') is monitored between two groups or situations to see what effects it has had. The two groups/situations are established in such a way that other factors are minimised. This gives rise to the need for *control* and *experimental* groups to be set up, where the experimental group experiences the effects of the independent variable. According to its proponents, experimental research, unlike descriptive survey methods and case study research, allows causal effects to be tested. Moreover, it can be predictive where the expected results of certain phenomena might be computed and tested against the observed pattern.

The model shown in Figure 3.3 is used by researchers in two ways:

(i) *When you wish to consider the effect of* x *on* y. You will require (at least) two groups – a *control* group, and an *experimental* or *treatment* group. Control groups are used to examine whether changes might not be taking place anyway (without the intervention), or whether there might be outside factors that might be studied. Different experimental designs reflect the many circumstances in which they are used.

(ii) *When you wish to examine whether you have significant changes over time.* For example, experimental designs allow intervention studies, whereby any group of individuals can be examined before intervention to provide baseline data, immediately after an intervention, and at subsequent points thereafter for 'follow up' data. This process allows you to identify if any change has taken place and if it persists.

However, before you start, you will need to consider the following points.

(a) Do you have easily available information about sufficient numbers of people or settings so that the data can be analysed statistically?

(b) Is there an opportunity to differentiate between (at least) two settings, or (at least) two groups of people? For example, you may wish to undertake some research which compares the performance of males and females, or examines the performance of two groups of children, one group of whom have been exposed to some new idea or stimulus.

(c) Are you able to match your subjects or groups on appropriate variables, for example, age, IQ, socio-economic status? This is important, as you need to ensure that any differences identified in your research are due to the factors being studied, rather than due to the characteristics of the groups. Matching on all variables is almost impossible.

The process of undertaking experimental research is presented in Figure 3.4. The figure indicates where appropriate different stages (e.g. hypotheses, analyses) are presented in more detail in this text.

Formulating a hypothesis

Hypotheses are statements that you wish to test. A hypothesis puts forward a considered view of the relationship between two or more variables. For example:

Method A of teaching maths is better than Method B

or

The introduction of health promotion clinics has had a significant effect upon the rates of coronary heart disease in this area.

Such views will be based on prior reading and on the interpretation of different views and opinions. However, you will need to test these views in a particular setting in order to establish whether such views can be substantiated by a research study.

In each situation you should be able to identify the *independent* and *dependent* variables at an early stage. From the above examples, the independent variable is that which you are testing through the introduction of a new method of teaching maths or of health promotion clinics. The effects of the independent variables will be recognised in the dependent variable (e.g. rate of coronary heart disease). Isolating one particular variable enables a test to take place to examine its effectiveness.

The research question *

Examine existing literature **

Formulate hypothesis ***

Design an experimental study ***

Conduct the study ***   ****

Analyse the results *****

Accept/reject your hypothesis *****

Implications for existing literature and knowledge and for further research ******

*	See Chapter 1
**	See Chapter 2
***	See sections within the remainder of this chapter
****	See Chapter 5
*****	See Chapter 6
******	See Chapter 7

Figure 3.4 Major stages in undertaking experimental research

In hypothesis testing you begin with a general hypothesis. Thereafter, you should consider two further aspects:

(a)   The general hypothesis must be operationalised into a format whereby it can be tested under experimental conditions. Each concept to be tested needs to be put into a format that can be measured. The specific sets of data that you use are referred to as *indicator variables* (i.e. they are indicative of a broader concept). It is important that you achieve content validity; that is, the indicator measures that which you wish to measure and not something else.

(b) You must write and test a *null* hypothesis. This is an unbiased statement that there is no significant relationship between the variables that you are examining, or that there is no effect of one variable upon another. Conventions for the wording of these hypotheses, and the examination of the hypotheses at levels of significance, will be considered in Chapter 6.

For example, each step may be presented as follows:

> *General hypothesis:* Smoking affects health.
> *Operational hypothesis:* There is a difference in the forced expiratory volumes of air between a group of 50-year-old males who are smokers and a group of 50-year-old males who are non-smokers.
> *Null hypothesis:* There is no significant difference in the forced expiratory volumes of air between a group of 50-year-old males who are smokers and a group of 50-year-old males who are non-smokers.

Designing an experimental study

Setting up the experimental design follows a number of stages:

(a) *Establishing hypotheses.* This culminates with the production of a null hypothesis.

(b) *Planning a test setting with experimental and control situations.* Independent variables will be tested in the experimental context, whilst dependent variables will relate to the control setting. Special attention should be given to the removal of extraneous variables (i.e. any outside influences that could affect the test). Variables can sometimes run out of control when other factors modify what is happening. In the first example presented earlier, the testing of maths schemes could be affected by different experiences at home, rather than by maths schemes at school.

(c) *Selecting your sample.* Which individuals will be selected? Are you utilising 'matched' groups, and comparing two such groups? If so, how will the groups be established?

Whether you are selecting geographical settings (e.g. comparing practice areas, or school catchment areas) or placing groups of individuals into control and experimental groups, there should be some means of 'matching' people or locations, whether, for example, by age, social class, intelligence (people) or socio-economic status, occupational profile or size (area). Matching groups can be problematic; despite much time and energy, many researchers have decided that this is impossible to do thoroughly.

(d) *Size of your sample.* In order to test your hypothesis rigorously you will need information from a representative sample of a size that will satisfy the demands of the statistical tests you want to use.

Three types of experimental design

These represent common approaches undertaken within experimental research. Whilst the second design is preferable there are often circumstances that demand attention to the other designs.

(a) *One group pretest–post-test.* In this situation testing of subjects takes place *before* and *after* some interventions. For example, a new curriculum project may be tested, or a new treatment in a clinical setting. The same group is tested at the beginning and end of the intervention. Whilst there are advantages in the retention of the same group of people, there are problems of assessing the influence of outside variables during the period between the initial and end tests.

(b) *Pretest–post-test control group design.* Two groups are established, and tested at an early stage to ensure that there is a match between the groups. One group is the control group, whilst the other is the experimental group. Variations can occur by the addition of further groups to the test situations. After the experience of the intervention in the experimental group there is a post-test to establish whether there is a significant difference between the experimental and control groups.

(c) *The quasi-experimental pretest–post-test design.* This is a variant of (b). In many real-life situations it is difficult to establish matched experimental and control groups. In these situations there is a compromise since it is difficult to assign people or settings to different groups at random. Whilst it assists the design if there is as close a match as possible, a perfect match may be very difficult to achieve. For example, if comparing schools or general practices, you may have to use two settings that may not be a mirror image of one another.

Conducting the study

A great deal of rigour must be attached to the collection of data. Whilst no natural setting can mirror that of the laboratory from which experimental research in the social sciences evolved, there is every reason for the hard-pressed researcher to be meticulous in the administration of the study and the handling of the data.

Much clinical research in psychology, medicine, nursing and paramedical subjects is based within the framework of experimental research. For some hard-pressed researchers it might appear the obvious research design to adopt. However, the research can be fraught with difficulties, and in some settings (e.g. hospitals) access to your preferred subjects for study (e.g. patients) is limited by practical and ethical considerations.

When conducting your experimental study, you may find it advantageous to have a mixed design in which you gather illustrative case study data in order to pay attention to the process of what is happening. Experimental research may be very good at producing a statistical result which may accept or reject a hypothesis, but, alone, it tells you little about the process underlying a causal relationship or significant variation in results between two groups of subjects.

Finally, you should be cautious in the wording of your conclusions. You need to be working with large data sets before considering generalisation. At best you should say that your data 'indicate...' or 'suggest...'.

Advantages of experimental research designs

- Researcher 'control' over the intervention(s) and over which subjects receive any intervention.

- Results are ensured.

- Reliable and well-respected research design.
- Individual factors can be identified.

Disadvantages of experimental research designs

- Problems in dealing with multiple causation; isolating individual factors may over-simplify complex issues.
- Ethical issues.
- Researcher bias and subjectivity in research design, methods and analysis.
- Hawthorne effect upon groups being researched (see Disadvantages of longitudinal research, this chapter).

The case study

Case study research belongs to a long tradition of research in the social sciences. It also has an equally important but slightly different set of origins within the medical and related sciences. It is therefore important that we distinguish between these two notions of case study.

   (a) Case study in the social sciences is used to allow a fine-tuned exploration of complex sets of inter-relationships. The case may be an individual, a group, an institution. The way a carer copes with a disabled spouse would be a focus of this kind of case study.

   (b) Case study in the medical and related professional disciplines is more commonly seen as a study of an individual case as an intervention occurs. The monitoring of a behaviour modification programme in psychotherapy would be an example of this.

While medical case studies provide very useful data, they form such an accepted part of the professional practice of those who utilise them that we shall not be looking at this form of case study. Instead we shall focus on the social science model of the case study in practitioner research. We shall look at ethnography as a specific research approach later in this chapter. In this section we shall examine cases and their structure and recognise that they can be used in research projects that are not purely ethnographic.

Definition of the case

The case is a unit of analysis: it can be an individual, a family, a work team, a resource, an institution, an intervention. Each case has within it a set of inter-relationships which both bind it together and shape it, but also interact with the external world. Stake usefully describes a case as 'an integrated system' and is careful to include selfhood in his definition (Stake, 1994). Identification of the boundary of a case can, however, cause concern at times. For example, when looking at a child as a case it is often impossible to focus on the child without becoming interested in and collecting information about the family or the institution in which the child is being educated or treated. In an examination of the inter-relationships within a case it is therefore possible to reveal not only internal elements of the case (the child), but also aspects of the context (the family, institution) in which the case is situated and indeed the policy and political contexts in which the family and institutions are, in turn, located. For these reasons cases provide fascinating and frequently complex insights into a time and place.

The uses of case study in research designs

Cases are used in a variety of ways in practitioner research. Their use will depend considerably on the research approach taken. For example, a case can be used to *explain* or illustrate a set of general principles; it can be the object of study in its own right, allowing a detailed and informative *description* of a particular phenomenon; or it can be the *exploratory* starting point for an experimental study and used as a way of clarifying the hypothesis to be selected. We shall look briefly at some of the uses made of case studies in social science research.

At their most simple, cases can be used *to explain* or illustrate aspects of the complexity evident in more general findings. When used in this way, cases are selected as examples of particular groups or categories and subsequent discussion of these cases can be related to, for example, survey data from a more extensive sample. In an explanatory or illustrative case a female school leaver who has had few formal examination successes and whose parents are not in employment can be presented as an example of how this particular sub-group of young people deals with the transition from secondary school. Themes evident in survey data from a larger and more general sample of school leavers can be exemplified in the particular experiences and understandings held by a small set of cases representing the sub-groups found in the larger sample. In this way case study brings to life the research findings and allows the voices of participants to be heard.

However, the sampling procedure for the selection of illustrative cases needs to ensure that cases are selected on the basis of their capacity to represent proportionally specific groups within the wider sample. For example, if a larger sample of 92 school leavers consists of 32 female and 60 male adolescents, 28 young people from homes where the parents are not in employment and 64 from homes where at least one parent is in full-time employment, and 42 adolescents from School A and 50 from School B, an illustrative set of case studies needs broadly to represent the various proportions of the features of the extensive sample.

A similar *explanatory* use of case study can be found in its use in evaluation studies to allow an examination of the processes of change. An evaluation of an intervention which relies on survey data from before and after the intervention can be considerably enhanced by the inclusion of some case studies of the intervention process which examine what the intervention actually meant in the lives of the participants as it occurred. Again careful sampling of cases is important.

A more complex use of case study to *explain* involves using cases to reveal patterns and themes in systems. Explanation here occurs as a result of the comparison of cases. Cases may appear to be similar or quite different from each other, their selection will depend on the contribution that they are expected to make to wider understandings about larger groups of cases and therefore on the research questions. One purpose of the comparison of cases is to generate or develop theory/theorising about the focuses of the cases. For example, a comparison of different cases would be appropriate when looking broadly at a national curriculum innovation in primary schools where cases might include head teachers, class teachers, pupils, parents, training providers and policy makers. A comparison of similar cases would serve a more focused enquiry into how, for example, non-specialist class teachers are making sense of the implementation of the curriculum innovation.

Cases can also be mainly *descriptive*. Though, importantly, any description will require focus and therefore the theoretical framing that prevents it becoming an unformed mass of indiscriminately collected data. The important distinction here between explanatory and descriptive cases is that while the importance of explanatory case studies lies in their capacity to represent wider themes and patterns, the focus of interest in a descriptive case lies in the case itself and its own very particular features. The intention is not to theory build or illustrate but simply to understand better a specific case, for example, this service innovation, health promotion initiative, community centre, or management team. The study may raise questions which deserve further exploration but raising questions is not its prime purpose. A descriptive case is particularly attractive when trying to examine complex phenomena such as the introduction of an innovation involving a number of professional groups.

The third broad approach to case study can be characterised as the *exploratory* case. Exploratory cases can be found in a number of different types of research design as an initial mapping of the terrain. Case study as a fresh look at the area of study is frequently used prior to a survey, an experimental study or a piece of action research. Exploratory cases which are used to gather information about a field of study are closer in purpose to descriptive cases than to explanatory cases. They aim at gaining insights into the area of study before clarifying the research focuses and attempting work with a larger sample or an intervention.

Indeed, we would argue for exploratory case study to be a compulsory feature in most research which is designed to enlighten us about practice and the situations in which it occurs. Good practitioner research has to start with an examination of practice and its context so that real issues can be addressed in the research project. One difficulty about being a practitioner researcher is that you are often so close to the focus of your study that you are unable to recognise some of its facets and as a result may design a study which does little more than confirm your prejudices. A fresh and systematic look at the field of study is therefore a healthy starting point. Whether or not case study becomes a major feature of your research design, our advice to you is to undertake at least a small case study as the starting point for your project.

Case study is not an easy option (as will be all too apparent when we look at data analysis in Chapter 6), but it gives us insights into social worlds that cannot be achieved in other ways and is therefore often well worthwhile. Importantly, explanatory, descriptive and exploratory uses of case study all develop out of careful theorising of the research project. Practitioner researchers need to be clear at the outset why they are using case study. Clarity when starting to design the research project will help when deciding how many cases are to be constructed, when they are to be compiled and the time scale for the analysis of case study data. Attempting to answer these questions early in the design process will save you valuable time later.

Case study can be time-consuming. The focus on meanings and the complexity of inter-relations that provide a rationale for case study demands high quality data. Our advice to you is to heed that offered by Bromley (1986) that good case study depends upon the best information available. We would stress the words *best* and *available*. You do need good quality interview and/or observational data, but as a practitioner researcher you cannot do the impossible; you can only work with what is available. Useful data sources for case studies, in addition to the interviews and observations we discuss in Chapter 5, include:

- documentation, for example, minutes of meetings, information written for service users, school inspection reports etc.,
- archival records, for example, previous surveys, information on service take-up, examination results etc.,
- evidence from physical artifacts, for example, plans of the institution demonstrating ease of communication, systems for curriculum planning and pupil assessment, photographs of the condition of the parents' waiting room etc.

Design of the case study

The first issue that you have to face in case study research is that the very labelling of an event or phenomenon as a case, and your presence as the observer of the case, will in fact change it. One way round this is to operate as a participant covert observer. But there are considerable ethical problems if that stance is taken by the practitioner researcher. The other way is to accept that you will disturb the case, name it and note it.

The second issue is how to deal with what many critics of case study describe as its soft subjectivity. Case study, however, is not a soft option. It has its own rigour and should be judged on its own terms. Central to the rigour of case study is the notion of triangulation.

Triangulation is what it sounds: a three-point perspective on an event or phenomenon. It can occur in several ways in practitioner research. The most common are:

- the use of several methods to get a purchase on the case,
- the gathering of information from several participants in the case,
- the use of more than one researcher to gather information on the case.

Most practitioner researchers will use a mixture of these forms of triangulation to gather a set of data that respect the multiple perspectives which are usually found within and around cases.

Figures 3.5, 3.6 and 3.7 exemplify how a practitioner researcher may design a case study of an event or series of events. There are other forms of triangulation; these include triangulation over time (looking at the same events over a period of time – recognising

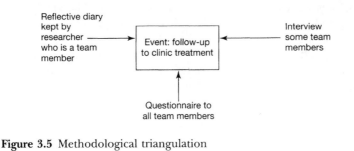

Figure 3.5 Methodological triangulation

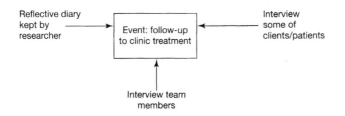

Figure 3.6 Participant or hierarchical triangulation

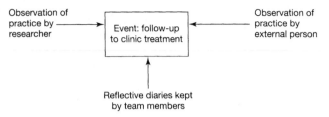

Figure 3.7 Researcher triangulation

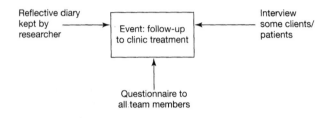

Figure 3.8 Mixed triangulation

that they will change over time) and theoretical triangulation (applying a variety of different theory-based questions to the event).

In practice what usually occurs is a mixture of Figures 3.5 and 3.6 in which at least two methods are used to get information on three perspectives on the event. Most practitioners have difficulty enlisting the help of another researcher, though group or team research helps to overcome this. An example of mixed triangulation is presented in Figure 3.8.

Advantages of case study

• It allows in-depth focusing on shifting relationships.

• It captures complexities.

• It allows a focus on the local understandings and sense-making of participants in the case and an opportunity for the voices of participants to be heard.

• It provides readable data that bring research to life and are true to the concerns and meanings under scrutiny.

Disadvantages of case study

- It can be an unwarranted intrusion into the lives of others.

- It is situation and time bound.

- It requires carefully collected, high-quality data.

- Appropriate data collection takes time.

- The researcher can become so immersed in the case that data analysis becomes difficult.

Progressive focusing designs

Designs that are described in this section owe their origin to the discipline of sociology more than to psychology. Observations are the main methods used, although interviews and diaries are also important. Observational methods are used in psychological research to examine the behaviours of both individuals and groups. Event and time sampling, which are described in Chapter 5, are examples of such methods. However, in this section we shall look at research designs which owe more to a process of progressive focusing as a result of the continuous analysis of observational fieldnotes. Again the actual methods are described in Chapter 5. This kind of research is often labelled ethnography.

The attention to the detail of both the actions and interactions of the objects of study, and to the context of these actions, that is demanded by ethnography can lead to it becoming overly descriptive if not done well. Good ethnography, however, offers theoretical or insightful descriptions which are informed by, and tested against, prevailing explanatory frameworks. These frameworks usually have their origins in the disciplines of sociology and anthropology. The frameworks themselves are also constantly open to questioning by the data. Consequently another important feature of this kind of design can be the development of theory. The work of Glaser and Strauss (1967) on grounded theory has been particularly influential in this respect. We shall return to this when we look at content analysis in Chapter 6.

Progressive focusing often depends upon a series of case studies in which the focus of observations is continuously refined as previous data are examined. Part of the data examination process is to allow fresh questions to be asked of the taken-for-granted and to enable the presentation of familiar events in new and challenging ways.

Ethnographic research design

Ethnographic research usually depends upon participant or at least unobtrusive observation. The researcher may be a participant in the action under observation but has as his or her primary purpose the observation of the action. This priority immediately presents a problem for some practitioners. A feature of participant observation is the opportunity to withdraw from the action to record the action and context in fieldnotes.

Ethnographic observations are usually used to gather data on a process. Care has to be taken over entry into the action so that observer effects on the context are minimal. While observing the action, attention is paid to detail, even trivialities, so that meanings can be teased out in later analyses.

Focusing occurs as the participant observer begins to identify key issues in observations. These might be centred on the rituals around entry and exit of children from a day care centre or the pattern of interactions evident in the behaviour of a head teacher. It is a research area in which it seems that expertise helps in the process of identifying the trees rather than the entire wood. Immersion in the phenomena is part of the research process, but at the same time the ethnographer needs to know how to create distance.

Another more obvious difficulty for practitioners who may be specialists in professions such as radiography or mathematics teaching, rather than sociology, is that sociological frameworks may not readily spring to mind while considering fieldnotes. It is of course possible to analyse fieldnote data in terms of, for example, children's conceptual grasp of mathematics, but this would render the study something other than ethnography to the purist. Ethnography has also been criticised for the subjectivity afforded the researcher in the choice of analytic framework. Should we, as an extreme example, apply a western, value-laden framework when examining fieldnote data gathered in West Africa?

Nevertheless the richness of data gathered and the questioning of professional assumptions allowed by this kind of study have provided useful and provocative insights into practice within several professions.

Advantages of progressive focusing

- Fresh perspectives are placed on the taken-for-granted.

- Rich and readable data are produced.

- Individuals are observed in interaction with the context in which they usually act.

- Local meanings are made public.

Disadvantages of progressive focusing

- Subjectivity in the choice of analytic frameworks.

- It is difficult to carry out ethnography on yourself.

- It may demand a good understanding of sociological, analytic frameworks.

- It is a difficult method for novice researchers.

Summary

Four different research designs have been presented. They form the basis for a large proportion of research studies undertaken by practitioner researchers on diploma or degree courses in education and the social sciences. Action research will be examined in more detail in the next chapter.

Remember, the research design gives the framework for both the research method and the means of analysis of the data produced by your research study. Each research question, practical considerations, and the environment in which you undertake your research will lend itself to a variation in the research design and methods adopted. There is no single method and design that can act as a catch-all for all studies. Rather, the emphasis should be upon the selection of a variety of techniques that will enable you to explore your research question in more detail, and provide greater weight to any generalisations that you feel able to make in your conclusions.

Further reading

Moser, C.A. and Kalton, G. (1977) *Survey methods in social investigation,* Heinemann. This is a useful introduction to and discussion about use of survey methods and their design.

Robson, C. (1994) *Experiment, design and statistics in psychology,* Penguin. Discusses the structure of experimental design, and related data analysis.

Stake, R. (1994) 'Case studies', in N. Denzin and Y. Guba (eds) *Handbook of qualitative research,* Sage, provides a well-argued analysis of some of the important issues in case study research.

Hamilton, D. (1994) 'Traditions, preferences and postures in applied qualitative research' also in Denzin and Guba (1994) is a clearly written and useful introduction to the labyrinth of debates around qualitative methods.

Hammersley, M. (1992) *What's wrong with ethnography?* Routledge. This is an excellent insider's critique of ethnography and the quantitative/qualitative divide.

Chapter 4

Action research

What is action research?

Action research in the UK developed, in part at least, in reaction to the increasing amount of research *on* teachers in the late 1960s and 1970s and a tendency to turn these professionals into objects of study in ways that did little for the teaching profession. Examples of action research work can now be found across a wide range of professional groups. Its popularity within the medical and related fields is a recent and developing phenomenon in the UK.

Any piece of research carried out by a practitioner which has, as its focus, the concerns of that practitioner's profession, can be defined as practitioner research. Action research is a sub-category of practitioner research. Practitioner research can only be designated action research if it is carried out by professionals who are engaged in researching, through structured self-reflection, aspects of their own practice as they engage in that practice.

Much practitioner research tends to be various forms of evaluation study. Again confusion can occur, this time between some more general types of evaluation and action research. A defining feature of action research is the central role of the *self-evaluating practitioner* in the research process. Evaluation studies which are carried out by people who are not themselves participating in the intervention which is under scrutiny, or studies which are carried out by participants but do not use reflective self-evaluation as a way of driving the evaluation, are not usually considered to be action research.

Another area of possible confusion is the overlap of terminology between reflective practice and action research. Clearly action research is carried out by reflective practitioners, but not all reflection on practice can be considered action research. Griffiths and Tann (1992) isolated five levels of reflective practice. These comprise two levels of reflection *in* action: (i) 'act – react' and (ii) 'react – monitor – react/rework – plan – act'; and three levels of reflection *on* action. Reflection *on* action includes: (i) a review process of 'act – observe – analyse – evaluate – plan – act'; (ii) a research process which they describe as 'act – observe systematically – analyse rigorously – evaluate – plan – act'; and (iii) a level they label 'retheorising and reformulation' which involves 'act – observe systematically – analyse rigorously – evaluate – retheorise – plan – act'. Of these only the last two levels of research and retheorising we feel may be easily regarded as action research. The categorisation of these activities as research is due to the systematic nature of observation, rigour of analysis and incorporation of theoretical frameworks into the analytic process in these two sets of processes of reflection *on* action.

This additional clarification may be open to debate, but it highlights an important element of action research and draws our attention to a distinguishing feature when comparisons are made between action research and simple careful reflection on practice. Action research involves more than thinking about what you have done. It includes drawing on relevant theory and the work of other practitioners, examining its relevance for your practice, and modifying widely held ideas to fit your practice. Ultimately it results in the emergence of your own right to be regarded as an informed expert practitioner who is able to make an important contribution to general public debate on professional issues.

Griffiths and Tann's final retheorising or emancipatory level of reflective practice is often considered the most important aspect of action research, as the confidence and knowledge gained by action researchers enable them to engage in informed and articulate ways in professional discourse and to help shape that discourse. It is of course not quite as simple as that, and we shall be looking at ways in which the processes and relationships involved in action research nurture and empower the professionals who undertake this way of working.

Cycles of enquiry in action research

We have looked at Griffiths and Tann's (1992) five levels of reflection. They argue that all five may need to be brought into play at different times if reflection on practice is to be effective. It would be useful to keep this suggestion in mind as we start to build up a picture of what an action research cycle may look like. It is easy to present attractively simple models. But most action researchers soon find these inadequate and want to develop their own cycles that actually match what they find themselves doing as they reflect in and on practice.

But let us start simply with a cycle of evaluation which is not strictly action research. The four-stage model of 'Where are we now?' 'Where do we want to get to?' 'How will we get there?' 'How will we know when we've got there?' is deceptive in its simplicity. It holds within it the important sequence of review, plan, act and review. It demands the detailed, if tentative, clarification of goals without which sound evaluation would be impossible. We can start to see the sequence in a cyclical form in the model shown in Figure 4.1. This much used sequence underpins good practice in a range of professions. It is, for example, central to the processes of teaching and medically related therapies.

Action research, however, adds an additional dimension to the evaluatory sequence by demanding systematic monitoring of the action taken. This monitoring includes, for example, observable changes, personal feelings and value positions, and often measurable outcomes. The general evaluation sequence becomes an action research cycle when data collection and reflective analysis of data are included within it.

The model now becomes Figure 4.2. As practitioners move through the cycle the review process becomes systematically

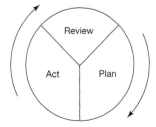

Figure 4.1 A simple evaluation model

Figure 4.2 An action research cycle

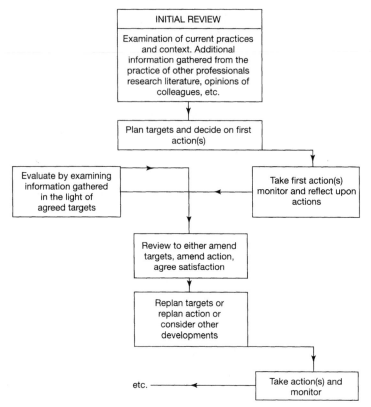

Figure 4.3 An action research cycle

based on information gathered while the actions being evaluated were actually undertaken.

Another variation on this model emphasises the relationship between action research and both case study and survey work. In Chapter 1 we suggested that action research can often follow on from case study or survey studies. Findings from both of these can raise issues that need careful testing in practice. In Figure 4.3 you can see that the starting point for the reflective cycle can be a survey or a detailed review of the current working context. This information may include related research by other researchers, the opinions of other practitioners and the detailed observations often found in case study work.

Figure 4.3 should be regarded as no more than a basic framework, as most action researchers find that smaller cycles of 'review, plan, act, review' are occurring within this larger framework. This is particularly the case within the stage we describe as 'take action(s), monitor and reflect'. You may find it a useful exercise, when you write up your study, to map your own model of action research based on the cycles in which you are actually engaged. Illustrative examples of what happened within these smaller, but important cycles, could also be provided.

Relationships in action research

Common misconceptions of the action researcher include the isolated practitioner engaged in either a cosy, less than serious, examination of his or her own navel or in agonising attacks of self-doubt as a result of seeing the process as self-destructive. Both pictures should be a long way from the reality.

For many action researchers the process of systematically gathering data about practice is a political one. Well-informed practitioners, armed with convincing data and articulate about the significance of elements of practice are able to deal with confidence with a world that is far from cosy. This level of confidence, however, can usually only occur if opportunities for talking about what is happening can be part of the process. Analytic conversations are an important element in action research. This is where we turn to the role of the *critical friend*.

The critical friend's purpose is to help to take the thinking of the action researcher onwards, so that the researcher, working from the information gathered, can begin to perceive new possibilities and developments.

As described so far the role sounds rather clinical. In reality action researchers often work together as groups of professionals who provide critical friend support for each other in mutually enhancing and self-affirming ways. Miller (1990, p. 115) quotes a teacher who found telling benefits from a support group.

> This group breaks down the isolation for me. I feel as though I am now part of a bigger picture. This gives me a chance to talk and think. I feel so much more confident as a teacher, as I realise that a lot of my frustration isn't all my fault. I share more readily and I'm not so resistant to others' ideas. ... I feel that this group is a bridge, letting me go back and forth from myself and this group to my larger worlds and then back again.

The movement back and forth, from a private to a more public domain, is an important feature of action research support.

If your tutor is also your critical friend, she or he may have to manage a difficult balance as the traditional tutor role has to be adjusted to new circumstances. In general, tutors who choose to encourage action research have thought out the dilemmas and provide enormous support. But as the relationship is a little different from many tutor–student relationships, not the least in expecting a great deal from the student, you need to ensure that your expectations do not include a certain degree of dependency on tutor decisions.

After trust, and acceptance of value positions, the key to the most effective form of dialogue for action researchers is good evidence as a starting point for discussion. Dialogues which focus on data, for example upon your observations or diary extracts, rather than half-remembered anecdote, place power in the interchange with the data collector and remove the need for apologetic forms of self-justification. Working from data, both or all participants are engaged in following the story told by the information given to them.

The action researcher as data-selector has considerable scope for self-editing and some do take up that option. Eventually, however, most action researchers feel that such a self-defensive approach is less than useful. The critical friend's role is to provide comfortable space and opportunity for the action researcher to clarify his or her own concerns and begin to move on to further action.

Data collection methods

Data collection methods for use by action researchers need to be easy to manage and non-intrusive for clients, to include opportunities for current reflection and to provide adequate information on the phenomena under scrutiny. A tall order! The answer is to use more than one method, in line with the way that we have discussed triangulation in Chapter 3.

There are, however, some important differences between data gathered for action research and those collected for other forms of research. While accepting that some of the data will be objective in, for example, counts of the number of times a resource is used or in the content analysis of written text, we need to recognise that seeking objectivity is less of an issue for action researchers than for other researchers.

This important difference is due to the centrality of the researcher's action to the research process in action research and the importance of his or her values and perceptions to the evaluation process. Consequently in action research if a set of actions actually produce the hoped-for outcome in, for example, the number of clients seen in one hour of clinic time, but still leaves the action researcher with a sense of disquiet, that unease becomes a legitimate focus for further study. Action research methods therefore need to provide opportunity for recorded reflections which include both objective and subjective data.

The list of data collection methods used in reflective enquiry is wide-ranging and ever-increasing as practitioners become more inventive in adapting established methods to suit specific situations. Consequently many of the methods discussed in Chapter 5 can be used if considered appropriate. We shall therefore in this section concentrate on a few examples of methods which seem to work particularly well for action researchers.

Reflective diaries

We have already emphasised in Chapter 1 the importance of keeping a research diary, and have indicated that information kept in a diary can be a legitimate source of data when discussing the evolution of a research study. The claim to legitimacy of data is even stronger for reflective diaries. A well-kept reflective diary can provide a major database for an action research study. You will remember that in Chapter 1 we also pointed out that action research studies are often reported within a structure that merges issues of research design, methodology and findings. The example of a structure for the final report of the study was one that separated the process into 'phases' and encourages a narrative but analytic style. Reflective diaries feed into this process and do more than the research diary we have already discussed, because they hold information that can be classified as findings. Extracts from reflective diaries should be included as appendices. Some researchers choose to submit the complete diary as an appendix, having numbered the pages for easy reference. It is a good idea to check what you should do with your tutor. Examiners differ in their feelings about the inclusion of complete diaries!

Keeping a reflective diary can be a taxing but rewarding experience as it demands and develops a high degree of self-exposure. You can, of course, limit that exposure so that it is self-exposure to yourself and not to a critical friend. This is done by maintaining the right to edit what is shared. But the extent of self-exposure, particularly as the process proceeds, can be personally very challenging and usually raises issues that researchers wish to discuss with a critical friend. In addition many users of diaries begin to perceive the diary itself as a source of support and another form of critical friend.

A reflective diary can be seen therefore as a conversation with yourself and will usually contain several of the following elements: an indication in some detail of what you intended to do that day or session and why; your perceptions of what happened (what the client did, how you felt, what else happened); your reflections on the targets you set or questions you explored in the light of what you noticed happening and what you intend to do next and why. Your perceptions and feelings are relevant as action research is essentially about making your practice effective.

The format of the diary is important because it shapes the use to which it can be put. We offer a framework as a starting point only as we emphasise that the diary is an entirely personal project and has to work for *you*. Figure 4.4 shows two facing pages in a notebook.

The diary pages may also be supplemented by press clippings, on-task observations, poems, photographs, diagrams, or any other relevant information. The basic format that we have suggested does, however, have some very useful advantages. Most importantly it allows for three stages of reflection. The first stage occurs as the events are reflected upon and those deemed most significant are selected and recorded in Section 1. A second level

| *Date*   *Location*
1.9.95   Science lab.

1. Recalled events written as recollections as soon as is possible. They will include descriptions and your responses both felt and intellectual. | 2. Questions raised to be tested in practice or against current understandings.

3. Implications for next actions/future practice. Intentions.

4. Leave blank and use the space for additional later reflections on reflections which may back up continuous themes evident elsewhere in the diary. |

Figure 4.4 The format of a reflective diary

of immediate reflection occurs and is worked out in Section 2 as initial interpretations are connected and compared with current research-based understandings. The third level of reflection is afforded by the use of Section 4. This section may be completed some time after the events recalled in Section 1. But it allows a tracing of common themes and patterns evident on different days across an action research cycle and presents an opportunity for enhanced self and contextual awareness.

Section 3 is important because it links reflection to action and provides the database essential to a project which is geared to the development of practice. Cross-referencing here to examples of other evidence, for example children's work or tape recordings, is often necessary.

The reflective diary is therefore both a data source and a structure which supports reflection on practice. You will probably find that the focus of the diary narrows as you progress with its use. In the early stages of your study what is recorded in Section 1 may be quite wide-ranging and diffuse as you clarify the focus of your study. As you move into action phases, informed by your considerations recorded in Sections 2 and 3, and even perhaps 4, your concerns will become more precise. Consequently the events recalled in Section 1 and reflected on later will be more sharply focused and probably contain more detail. Using the diary as a conversation with yourself will both help you record the focusing process and support you as you work through it.

Additional insight can be achieved if two or more of you use reflective diaries to examine the same event. The comparison of diaries can be fruitful in at least two ways. First, it leads you into useful discussion of different perceptions with colleagues, and secondly, it highlights for you both what you fail to observe and what is important for you in your professional decision making.

It is important that you draw intelligently on your reflective diary as you write up your project. To that end it is important to record the links between review and replan and to include quite specific detail. A discussion of detail leads us to an examination of methods of observation used by action researchers.

Observation in action research

Detailed observations can be used to supplement the material kept in a reflective diary. General observational methods will be covered in Chapter 5 and can be incorporated to great effect in action research studies. In addition to the more traditional methods of observation there is a wide range of observational activity that is undertaken by action researchers and it is the latter that we shall now examine.

It may be useful to see methods of observation placed on a continuum which starts with loose relatively unfocused observation and moves to tightly focused study of specific events. The selection of method from that continuum may depend upon where you are in the reflective or action research cycle. At the start of the cycle it may be appropriate to make general observations noting only what comes to your attention. The justification for this is that action research has to start with what is important for you in your practice. Later, as evaluatory targets are clarified, it will be necessary to use methods that allow close scrutiny of the impact of actions you take. We shall start with the least structured methods.

Looking and seeing

An important starting point for any practitioner research is an awareness, if not a complete understanding, of what is going on. The first step may be to take 30 seconds or a minute out from your normal interactions and look at what is going on. You should write down what you see, even include any comments that come to mind. Later your jottings can be placed in your reflective diary. The extract in Figure 4.5 from the observations of a nursery assistant, originally written on the back of an envelope, illustrate the technique. Later that day on the reverse side of the envelope

```
No children at water
why?
lots of sand
K & T at sink washing up
splashing
Tray in corner
Dark. Difficult to get to
Toys in cupboard
.........................................
.................. etc.
```

Figure 4.5 An initial observation

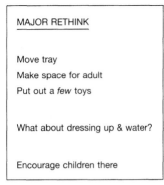

Figure 4.6 Reflections on observations

she wrote the notes shown in Figure 4.6. These notes indicate the start of a reflectively research-based approach to improving practice and, as a resource for a written project, belong in a reflective diary.

Another commonly used form of relatively loose observation is the review method. Here an early years teacher, for example, may take time out to list which of those activities chosen by children at free choice time can be designated science and who is engaging in them. Carried out over several days the review would indicate the curriculum experience of children, and areas in which teacher action may be necessary. In this example a proforma may be useful for each observation session. In the example given in Figure 4.7 the first two columns would be completed while the activities were under way and all activities would be noted regardless of their immediate relation to science. The analysis found in the third column would be made soon after the session.

Focusing the looking

The next stage for action researchers is often to maintain the open-endedness of the review methods we have just described, but narrow the focus to a specific issue. If initial observations have highlighted a concern it may be necessary to examine that area in some detail before deciding on the action to be taken. We have already stated that practitioner concerns or feelings, however difficult to articulate, are legitimate starting points for action research. If, for example, you have a feeling that in informally structured work with children or clients some are getting more attention than others, you may want to monitor

Time from to		
Activity	Children at activity	Science? attainment target –level?

Figure 4.7　A review proforma

what happens over a few sessions to see whether your hunch is based in reality. Again some kind of proforma may be useful (see Figure 4.8). But it may be more appropriate simply to keep rough jottings and transfer the information to a proforma at the end of the session. You could then add additional observations and reflections on the events. Several proformas could then be compared, goals set and actions planned.

　Photographs also provide useful focused observational material, but may be inappropriate for use by professionals who need to

Time from to	
Contact with	Reason

Figure 4.8　A focused review proforma

have regard to client privacy. Having decided on the general focus of the exploration, for example, a midday meal in a day centre, it is important that the researcher selects a sampling focus before picking up the camera. In the example given, the sampling focus could be either a table of lunchers or one person or a member of staff. The photographs should then be taken at one-minute intervals over an appropriate period of time, perhaps five or ten minutes. The prints can then be examined in order of occurrence as a form of time sampling (see Chapter 5). This is a particularly useful exercise for a group of colleagues who are using action research methods, as photographs provide a powerful stimulus for discussion.

As you move on, through the cycle of action research to 'the taking action(s) and monitoring stage' (Figure 4.3) the concern is the need to examine, in some detail, the effects of the innovations made. Detail is very important at this stage as the strength of many action research studies depends upon the close observation that takes you to the insights that make such researcher enquiry worthwhile.

You may find that the target child method given in Chapter 5 is a useful technique as it can be adapted to a range of contexts and 'targets'. Or you may wish to video events. Some action researchers dislike the semi-structured approach provided by the target child method, others find that the disadvantages of videoing (particularly knowing when to stop the analysis) outweigh the advantages.

By far the most popular method used is a less structured variation of the target child method. This method requires the researcher to make detailed observations at specific moments of importance
to create what we describe in Chapter 5 as vignettes of an event.

The information in Figure 4.9 could be analysed using a simple form of content analysis by starting with two lists: 'What J can do', 'What J can't do'. These lists can then be further analysed by, perhaps, listing achievements that were new or surprising and those that were not. J's inabilities can be treated in the same way. That very basic categorisation will enable you to isolate successes in your work, link your actions with J's and identify areas for development. What is crucial is that you note what is important and work from your observations in order to develop your practice.

We mentioned earlier in this chapter that smaller cycles of reflective evaluation will be occurring as you work at the 'take

```
                                    Date:      Time:
                                  _____

  J and B arrived 5 mins late.
  B in vest and shorts – but clean.
  J apologised. Said she had to wait at post office.


  Making soup. J confused cabbage and carrot and thought they
  cost 3 or 4 times more than they do.
  She cut up veg and washed them carefully.
  Asked me for salt and pepper. Added it herself.
```

Figure 4.9 Examples of focused observation

action(s), monitor and reflect' stage indicated in Figure 4.3. The detail that informs these smaller hourly or daily cycles needs to be recorded and its part in the developing process made clear when the full story is told.

Audio-taping

The use of a tape recorder is a common feature of action research. Like observations it can be used for different purposes at different times in the research cycle. At the review stage it may be appropriate to use the tape simply to listen to yourself with a group of children or a client in order to start to consider areas for improvement. Later in the cycle you may wish to focus on specific elements in your interactions, or you may wish to use the recorder to provide information on situations that would change were you to be physically present, for example, pupils' use of scientific language in paired work. Tape recording can also be used to supplement some observational techniques. Any observational method that involves time sampling (see Chapter 5) can be analysed alongside a tape recording of the interactions under scrutiny as tape scripts can be segmented into compatible time segments. Nevertheless, the apparent simplicity of this method of data collection can mask the potential pitfalls listed in Figure 4.10.

Extracts from recordings can be written up ready for analysis and used as illustrative material. The time taken for this part of the exercise does need to be taken into account when planning your own time management. The tips in Figure 4.10 that urge immediate listening and additional commentary together with moderation in the quantity you collect do need heeding.

DON'T	DO
• Record interactions of groups of more than 3 unless simply focusing on one member in that group. • Try to record without testing sound quality. • Record too much, you have to listen to it and analyse it. • Be put off if it doesn't work well the first time.	• Listen to the tape and make additional notes <u>as soon as possible</u> after recording. • Use the best quality machinery you can and attempt to buffer interference by working in a carpeted area or by putting recorder on a cushion. • Carry batteries with you. Sockets are not always convenient. • Try it out in small ways first.

Figure 4.10 Tips for tape-recording

Ethical issues in action research

In Chapter 1 we indicated that action research raised specific ethical concerns. The methods we have been discussing demand both self-awareness and in some cases a degree of invasion of the privacy of others. Invasion of privacy is increased if you are attempting to tell the story of group action research. The ethical guidelines we suggested in Chapter 1 apply here, but it may also be necessary to spend time, before the project starts, to create ground rules that are agreed by all concerned. The following points may provide a useful checklist of topics to be covered in the discussion.

- Who 'owns' the data gathered?
- Do individuals have the right to edit data from reflective diaries?
- Can an individual have the right to veto the publication of any material?
- What safeguards for privacy need to be built in?
- What about the clients' rights?
- Other situation-specific issues.

When you have worked your way through a, doubtless lengthy, consideration of these issues to reach an agreement on behaviour, you need to ensure that the ground rules are recorded and confirmed by everyone.

Telling the story

We started this book by describing research as a quest for better understanding of events. A good record of the process of that quest is perhaps more relevant to action research than to the other designs we describe, as action research findings constantly redirect design and method.

Capturing the rigour and excitement of action research in a formal written report can be problematic unless the writing process is given the weight it deserves. It is therefore essential that the write-up is approached as an analytic narrative which is backed by sound data. But more of that in Chapter 7.

Using action research in organisational development

We have already indicated that one frequent outcome of action research is a growth in professional confidence which parallels the increased understanding of the workplace that comes with careful reflective enquiry. We have also suggested that key elements in the reflective enquiry process are planning, evaluation, communication, trust and the confronting of difficulties or problem solving. In addition, although we have not made it explicit, we have implied that ownership of change comes through involvement in identifying, planning, enacting and, particularly, evaluating that change.

Action research in the United Kingdom emerged from the work of Lawrence Stenhouse in a humanities curriculum development project based in secondary schools in the 1970s. Consequently much of the initial rationale of action research is given in curriculum development terms. Stenhouse, in his premise that there can be no curriculum development without teacher development, firmly tied the enhancement of practice and context to the individual learning processes of practitioners. In addition his claim that by understanding schools better teachers would be able to change them, similarly joined together issues of communication, professionalism and organisational development.

It is the organisational development aspect which is more widely applicable to a range of professional groups. Many of the key features of action research are also essential elements of person-centred methods of organisational development. Any

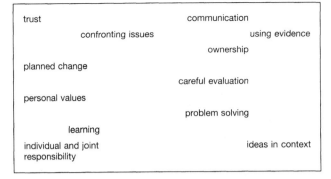

Figure 4.11 Key features of action research and organisational development

analysis of both sets of literature will identify the common features shown in Figure 4.11.

Because of this similarity, action research is frequently incorporated into staff development programmes which support institutional development. A common example of such an approach can be seen in Figure 4.12.

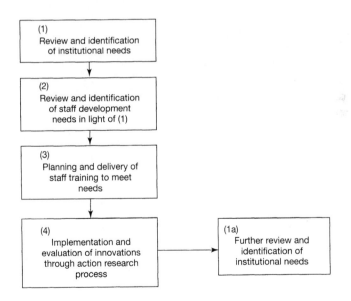

Figure 4.12 The incorporation of action research into staff development planning

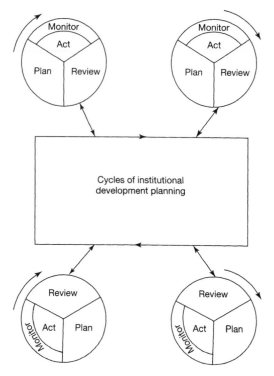

Figure 4.13 The incorporation of action research into institutional development planning

Figure 4.13 shows how the action research cycle may also be incorporated into long-term institutional development planning. While the institutionalisation of action research is a very attractive way forward, and may indeed be what has led you to an interest in reflective enquiry, it does raise questions, the most important of which is that of ownership of the change process.

Action research usually starts with a lengthy review and focusing period in which development points are identified and ways forward planned by the practitioner-action takers. If that element of the process is hijacked by those who want to impose their own goals on practitioners, the process is fundamentally changed. Action research may then simply be promoted as a way of ensuring that practitioners obediently self-monitor their attempts to achieve goals that are entirely externally imposed. If that happens the personal and professional development gains we have identified will be lost. We are not suggesting that external constraints or opportunities should not be addressed or even become central to the enquiry process. Rather we are proposing that initial agreement to the action to be taken needs to be reached in ways which engage participants as professionals in institutional development concerns. The importance of personal values to action research, as we have been describing it, is a distinguishing feature. Without attention to personal values, action research becomes a different and less transforming exercise.

One way of ensuring that institutions and individuals gain as much as possible from the effort of action research is to base the commitment to action research in a partnership or research network which includes membership from higher education research communities. Writing about such networks in educational settings, Huberman makes forceful claims for the capacity of systematic networks which draw on the research-based insights of higher education specialists to inform and improve practice (Huberman, 1995). Edwards and Collison have made similar claims in the context of teacher training partnerships between schools and universities (Edwards and Collison, 1996).

Professionals who are working in contexts which are constantly changing as a result of external pressures need to feel that they have some control of at least aspects of their own professional lives. For some people action research becomes a way of maintaining that professional control and self-awareness while making those adaptations to practice that are deemed necessary. For this reason action research can underpin programmes of staff development. Teams of teaching colleagues engaged in systematic enquiry into ways of modifying assessment practices so that they can cope with larger groups of students would be an example of this activity.

Those of you who are attracted to action research as a form of staff and therefore institutional development need to address the issues we are starting to raise and should avoid a simplistic acceptance of the easy fit of action research to staff development in every type of institutional climate. There may, for example, be difficulties in encouraging the self-exposure essential to reflective enquiry if action research cycles are incorporated into quality control mechanisms in a hierarchically controlling institutional structure.

Use your imagination

We have just begun to touch upon important aspects of action
research in order to alert you to issues you may want to pursue.
These topics may include applications of the process, values and
research or the relationship between research and learning. You
may, alternatively, wish to give little emphasis to these more
complex concerns and focus at a more functional level on the
development of your own practice. Wherever your interest
might be, action research gives you scope for inventiveness and
creativity. This assertion is as true of attempts to incorporate
systematic enquiry into institutional quality assurance systems as it
is of adapting an observational method to suit the constraints of
your workplace and the time you have available.

Action research is premised on the reciprocity of individual
and context as ideas held by practitioners are tested and developed in the workplace. As a mode of enquiry it is itself constantly
developing. This adaptation occurs as effective practitioners
engage in and develop the potential and techniques of the
enquiry process in an increasingly wider range of professional
contexts. While we would not advocate the notion that 'action
research is what you want it to be' we would suggest that you
should, tentatively, review, plan, act and review any innovation in
this model of enquiry.

Further reading

A great deal has been written about action research.

Lawrence Stenhouse's 1975 text was the UK starting point and
therefore has to be mentioned: Stenhouse, L. (1975) *An introduction
to curriculum research and development*, Heinemann.

John Elliott has taken these ideas on to link them with school
development and his perspectives are proving influential with other
professional groups. Elliott, J. (1991) *Action research for educational
change*, Open University Press.

Elliott's book does give some practical help with research methods, but
perhaps the most comprehensive practical guide to action research is
Hopkins, D. (1993) *A teacher's guide to classroom research*, Open
University Press. Again, although this is written for teachers it can
give practical help to any action researcher.

Jean McNiff has written several books based on her own action research. Her writing therefore carries the conviction of the committed action researcher. McNiff, J. (1993) *Teaching as learning*, Routledge, is such a personal account.

Other texts at a more theoretical level include Carr, W. and Kemmis, S. (1986) *Becoming critical: knowledge and action research*, Falmer Press.

Educational Action Research is a journal published by Triangle which contains accounts of action research studies in a range of professional fields.

Chapter 5

Selecting the method

Starting points

Of equal importance to selecting the right research question and deciding on the design of the study, is selecting the methods of enquiry you will use. When choosing your research methods you need to be able to answer yes to each of the following questions.

- Is this method going to get the kind of information I need?
- Can I be sure that I'm building up as accurate a picture of the event(s) I am studying as I possibly can?
- Can I manage to do this with the people concerned in the time available?

These three questions can be seen as a series of research issues that need to be addressed very early in an enquiry process. These issues can be summarised as concerns about validity, reliability and feasibility and each will be discussed in turn before looking in detail at specific methods.

Validity

The validity of the information you gather is seen in the extent to which your methods pick up what you expect them to. For example, teachers' responses to questions on a questionnaire about how to teach may not be a valid indication of how they actually do teach in classrooms. You would find out about how teachers teach by watching them at work. Testing children's performance on curricula they have not experienced would similarly be an invalid measure of their potential as learners.

You need to ask a simple question as a practitioner when considering validity, 'Is what I'm finding out making sense?' In other words, 'Do my data have face validity?' Face validity would be lacking if in interviews all teachers in your sample talked about the virtues of interactive group work in classrooms but you knew that they largely used whole-class teaching methods. Similarly, if the bright and enthusiastic youngsters you teach all scored badly on a test you would have to query the validity of the test as a measure of their potential for learning. There are other indications of research validity, but the hard-pressed researcher needs to deal primarily with the common-sense concerns around face validity.

Reliability

One definition of reliability suggests that measures or data collection methods should be uninfluenced by changes in context. This is certainly an important concern when you are dealing with detailed educational or medical assessment devices, or gathering survey data. But even here there has always to be the recognition that mood and context will have effects.

Reliability is an even more complex concern when we turn to gathering data in and about the messy and constantly changing contexts in which we all work. As practitioners you are usually positioned in the work context and are changing it by asking questions about it. You cannot expect your questions to be interpreted in the same way week after week in different situations. Different contexts will have different histories and your probings will elicit different perspectives and even different concerns.

Reliability in terms of consistency cannot therefore always be a goal. Reliability in terms of getting the best information available and building up as rich and complex a picture should be.

As practitioners we are only too aware of the complex sets of interactions that constitute a workplace, the wide range of perspectives on the interactions and number of possible ways of interpreting them. We need to get some kind of grip on these shifting sets of reality without losing the richness that such a picture offers. The discussion of triangulation in Chapter 3 is one example of how reliability issues can be addressed in, for example, case study research.

Feasibility

The first thing you must promise yourself when you start on a piece of research is that you will finish it. So we start with some health warnings which if heeded should help your general well-being.

Don't

- Gather too much data from too wide a range of sources: you'll end up with superficiality.

- Gather too much data: you'll never have time to analyse it.

- Commit yourself to gathering data from sources which haven't yet agreed to help you or might be upset by your enquiries.

- Forget that data collection is only part of the process: reading, analysis and writing up all take much longer than collecting the information.

Do

- Be focused and gather *only* the information you need.

- Work out a realistic time-scale *before* you start.

- Check that other people really know what you want from them and are willing to co-operate.

- Remember that you have family, friends, a job, and that research is only part of life.

We shall be looking at the advantages and pitfalls related to feasibility of each information collection method we are examining later in this chapter. For example, an in-depth interview can take at least an hour, take four hours to type if you are a fast typist, produce 30 pages of typescript and take days to analyse. Could you get the information you need from an attitude scale?

If you find that your study isn't feasible it may be necessary to reconsider the research question. It is better to discover this *before* you start!

Which method?

As you will have already gathered we are avoiding categorising methods as appropriate to either a quantification exercise or to a more qualitative form of analysis. We will simply take each method in turn. We will examine what each has to offer, and how to develop and use it. The corresponding methods of analysis will be covered in Chapter 6. Nevertheless, we will urge you to be mindful of the demands of analysis as we proceed.

Survey methods

It is often useful to see the events you are examining as like an onion with its various layers offering different levels of understanding of what is going on. If we keep this image in mind survey methods give access to the outer layers. Questionnaires will give you a good picture of the surface elements, such as average age or country of origin. Attitude scales will take you below the surface to examine feelings towards events, but neither method could be described as probing or providing rich sources of data in which the voices of the participants are heard. The centre of the onion is reached with interviews, which we shall examine later in the chapter. Sampling is important in survey research so refer to Chapter 3 to check sampling procedures.

Questionnaires

<table>
<tr><td>

Advantages of questionnaires

- They give useful background information.

- They can be administered by post or to a lot of people at the same time in one setting.

- They are reliable and can be administered before and after an intervention.

</td></tr>
</table>

<table>
<tr><td>

Disadvantages of questionnaires

- Recipients don't like them.

- The descriptive data they produce rarely allow you fully to demonstrate your skills of analysis.

</td></tr>
</table>

- You often need to chase up non-returns to ensure that your sample is appropriate.
- They give only quite superficial information.

If despite this discouragement you want to use a questionnaire you need to ensure that it is focused, short and easy to analyse.

Stages in writing a questionnaire

1 Take a blank piece of paper and write your research question in the middle of it.

2 Brainstorm and write down on the paper the types of information you need in order to answer the research question, for example age, qualifications, experience.

3 Group the brainstorm areas: for example career issues, domestic issues, practice issues, and place them in order. Put simple questions first and more searching questions later.

4 Look at them again. Do you really need *all* that information? Is there overlap?

5 Start to write the questions. Avoid negatives (and double negatives!). Have only one idea in each question: for example 'Do you find your work difficult and challenging?' could produce No and Yes as an answer from respondents. Think whether you want closed Yes–No questions or more open questions. If you want open questions use 'Why', 'What', and 'How' questions. For closed questions use 'Is' and 'Do'.

6 Begin to think about analysis as you write. Open-ended questions produce written answers which take time to analyse. Closed questions may not be simply Yes or No but may require you to set up categories of response, for example please tick the box that shows your age.

20 or less	21–30	31–40	41 or more

You may also wish people to tick or underline their own responses from a list you provide or even rank order the frequency of use of, for example, a service you provide.

7 Try to avoid response set which may come in a long run of Yes–No questions, such as:

  are you a nice person?
  are you kind to children?
  are you cruel to animals?
  are you considerate of the elderly?

8 Check that there is a logical progression in the order of the questions.

9 Try to keep the questionnaire short. Two pages maximum is a reasonable guide. Above all try to keep it simple.

Attitude scales

First of all you need to be clear how an attitude scale differs from a straightforward questionnaire. An attitude scale is a list of statements to which we ask people to respond by showing the extent to which they agree or disagree with a statement. For example:

	Strongly disagree			Strongly agree
Doing practitioner research is fun	_____	_____	_____	__✓__

A questionnaire collects simpler, more descriptive data about, for example, what people do or have done.

Alternatively, you may use the *semantic differential technique* and ask for responses to a statement such as

Designing a study as a practitioner researcher is

Easy _ _ _ _ _ _ _ Difficult

Respondents indicate their attitudes to the statement by marking a point on the seven-point scale and responses are scored from $+3$ on the positive side to -3 on the negative side. A series of similar statements about aspects of practitioner research on a rating sheet could indicate a practitioner's attitude towards evidence-based practice. When using semantic differentials it is essential that the descriptors (e.g. easy–difficult) are opposites and do offer a distinct dimension (see Oppenheim, 1992). Responses to individual items (e.g. designing a study) can be averaged so that the attitudes of distinct sub-groups may be compared. Oppenheim warns that if several concepts are to be examined, several separate rating sheets should be used. For example, if we were looking at evidence practice and youth work the separate rating sheets might ask the respondents to focus on evidence-based practice in the first rating sheet and then on the professional status of youth workers in the second, even though some of the same items might appear in both rating sheets.

Advantages of attitude scales

• Attitudes sometimes indicate how people will behave.

• They provide data with which you can demonstrate your skills of data analysis.

• They do allow you to go below the surface of issues and yet keep your data numerical.

• They can be administered by post or to a lot of people at one time in the same setting.

• They are reliable-and can be administered before and after an intervention.

Disadvantages of attitude scales

• Attitudes are influenced by context and therefore don't always remain constant indicators of behaviour.

• They can be seen as yet another questionnaire and be unpopular with recipients.

• You may need to chase up non-returns to ensure that your sample is appropriate.

There are two main types of attitude scale: the Thurstone and the Likert Scales. They have similar reliability and the Likert Scale is much easier to compile. We provide a guide to their compilation. More attention is given to the Likert Scale which is our preferred choice.

Stages in compiling a Likert Scale

1 Decide on the focus on the scale and brainstorm around the focus.

2 Compile a short (10 to 15 minute) interview from the brainstorm.

3 Interview three or more people from the population (though not the sample) to whom you'll be giving the scale. Interviews are necessary to ensure that, as much as possible, you use the language used by the recipients in your attitude scale.

4 Return to your brainstorm and group the issues in the way described for a questionnaire.

5 Look at your interviews, match statements in the interviews to the issues in the brainstorm, see whether additional points are raised in the interviews, include them if they are useful or important to this interview sample.

6 Write out your attitude statements. Avoid negatives and double focus questions; for example avoid statements like 'The clinic is clean and welcoming'. It may not be both. Try to keep it short – a page to two pages in length.

7 Decide whether you want a five- or a four-point scale. Some people think that a five-point scale results in over-use of the third point. Others feel that a genuine mid-point response should not be denied the respondents.

8 Check the words on the scale. Can all your statements be responded to by 'strongly agree' to 'strongly disagree', or are they 'all the time' to 'none of the time', or 'a lot' to 'none' statements? Maybe you need to regroup some statements so that appropriate scales can be applied to specific sections of the instrument.

9 Write full and careful instructions (with examples).

10 You may also want some questionnaire information, for example, name, age or occupation. This may be particularly important as one easy way of using attitude scale data is to compare the attitudes of different groups to the same event.

What you cannot get from a Likert Scale is a general 'attitude towards' score for the whole scale. What you gain in simplicity of construction you lose in lack of sophistication of scaling.

Thurstone Scaling

To be able to get one measure of general attitude towards, for example, teamwork you would need to use a Thurstone Scale. In a Thurstone Scale a series of statements around a single subject is produced (e.g. attitudes to teamwork within the work setting) which present extremes at the two ends of support for teamwork. The production process is long and detailed but in summary, prior to your own survey, you should identify a group of 'experts' who can sort different statements about the focus subject into a preferred order of importance and create a standard scale. In the process some of the original statements may be discarded (e.g. because they are misleading). Once a reasonable number of statements (arguably at least twelve) are agreed you are able to produce a questionnaire. Respondents are then asked to indicate their agreement or disagreement with each individual item (e.g. 'teamwork produces a more efficient workforce'). Respondents are then assessed against the overall results of the standard scale and a final attitude score produced for each respondent. Further information on the important detail of Thurstone Scaling can be found in Oppenheim (1992) which is an excellent and up-to-date guide to the field of attitude measurement. However, it is important to remember that the procedure can be time-consuming and relies upon a high degree of commonality/ understanding between the original expert group and the respondents undertaking the survey.

Q Sorts

Q Sorts are very similar in basic construction to attitude scales, and particularly semantic differential techniques, but arguably allow for more individualised responses through a system of forced choice attitude mapping. They are particularly useful for examining the effects of interventions on individuals' self-perceptions, but can be put to a range of uses. More information on Q Sorts can be found in Cohen (1976).

Observational methods

If we return to the onion image used earlier when we introduced survey methods we should see observational methods as a way of accessing surface or outer layer issues, but with the potential to identify novel aspects and to raise new questions. We need to remind ourselves that observations can only pick up behaviours: they cannot reliably give us direct access to meanings and intentions.

All good practitioner research studies start with observations. It would be very difficult to identify a practitioner research question without first looking at aspects of practice. Much practitioner research aims at changing practice (and hence practitioner behaviour or client behaviour). How better to check the changes than by observing the behaviour in some systematic way? Different reasons for observing demand different forms of observations and subsequent recording. Consequently there is a wide range of observational methods available to the practitioner researcher.

Observational methods include the following: pre-prepared checklists for review purposes, open-ended but strictly timed tightly focused target methods and also loosely narrative vignettes or critical incidents. The selection of method may depend on its use within the cycle of research activity; whether identifying the research question or checking the outcomes of an intervention. Equally it may depend whether you want illustrative narrative data or countable evidence of, for example, frequency of behaviours.

But before we examine each of the main methods used by practitioners let's look at some key features of reliable observations:

- Only write or note what you see, *not* what you think a behaviour might imply (people smile from embarrassment as well as from pleasure).
- Don't write or note what you don't see. You can identify gaps in expected behaviour when you analyse the data. To say, for example, 'not smiling' or 'not interacting with others' is unnecessary and may put too much emphasis upon your expectations of behaviour in the recorded data.
- Try to capture the behaviour in context. What else is going on? What happened before and afterwards? Where is it taking place?
- Have a clear target. Don't try to look at too much at once or for too long. Observing demands tiring, highly focused concentration.

We shall now look in more detail at some observational methods. We shall start with the most closed and end with the most open methods and urge you to avoid equating high validity and reliability only with those methods at the most closed end of the methodological dimension.

Checklists and event sampling

Checklists usually include lists of behaviours or facilities that might be expected to be observed. The observer checks the existence of these and records appropriately in the list. These lists may give the opportunity for recording, for example, the extent to which a facility is available within specific·settings. Checklists are particularly useful when reviewing practice against a set of agreed criteria and are often a sound starting point for developing practice and provision.

Event sampling has some of the qualities of a checklist. It is a simple count of incidents. If you are trying to decrease the number of times one child leaves her seat in a session you would wish to count the number of times this occurs within a given period before you intervene with a behaviour-changing programme (baseline data) and again collect frequency data from an equivalent period at the end of the treatment or programme. Although this example is of a single child, event sampling is a particularly effective way of quickly recording the behaviour of a group of people over a given period as other methods of observation may prove too complex for that purpose.

The sampling usually happens in one of two ways. The most sophisticated of these is to use an 'event recorder'. At its most elementary this is a counter which records the number of times a behaviour occurs as the observer presses a button to register each occurrence. At its most complex the recorder is an electronic keyboard on which the frequency of occurrence of a range of behaviours may be recorded. The less sophisticated method of event recording is a checklist on which expected behaviours are listed and the frequency of behaviours is noted.

Advantages of checklists and event recorders

- They provide useful numerical baseline data.

- They are quick and reliable.

- They can be used to check outcomes.

- You can quite easily gather information about behaviours in groups of people.

Disadvantages of checklists and event recorders

- They don't record *when* events occur.

- You cannot view the event in context and see the antecedents and effects.

- You have to decide exactly what you are to look *for* before you start to look *at.*

- You may miss recording a lot of useful information through only focusing on the preselected event(s).

Time sampling

This is a complex area with a variety of formats available to researchers. Again, aware of the constraints on the busy practitioner researcher, we shall select from the array. Time sampling involves recording a behaviour at regular intervals. These may be as close as every 30 seconds or as far apart as every five minutes or hour. The methods used may include paper and pencil recording on a proforma, regular photographs, or video and audio tape recordings which then are themselves analysed on a time-sampling basis.

Time sampling should not be confused with event sampling, for although there are strong similarities the differences mean that it is used for very different purposes (Figure 5.1)

	Event sampling	Time sampling
Similarities	• You need a clear focus before you start. • You gather data that are or can be easily made numerical.	
Differences	• It provides frequency data. • You can gather information on several people at a time.	• It provides continuous data. • You (usually) gather information on an individual or very few people at a time.

Figure 5.1 The differences between event sampling and time sampling

---

Advantages of time sampling

- You get continuous data which allow you to look at antecedents and subsequent events.

- If you use small intervals you can gauge how long any behaviour lasts.

- The methods usually allow detailed focusing on a wide range of behaviours exhibited by an individual or small group.

- The methods can often be used to allow you to record sequences of interactions.

Disadvantages of time sampling

- You don't always get frequency data.

- It is difficult and tiring as it demands intense concentration.

- If you use predetermined recording systems you can miss important novel behaviours.

- If you don't use predetermined recording systems you need to analyse your observations very soon after making them.

All time sampling demands a clear observational focus, an agreed time interval at which the recording is made, a timer (a watch with a 60-second hand will do) and a prepared system of recording the actions being observed. There is a range of methods that employ these criteria.

Photographs

These are the easiest method. If taken at, for example, 60-second intervals over a period of 10 or 15 minutes they can provide useful rich information in an accessible form which can be constantly returned to.

Danger Points

- You need to be clear about your focus. Is it a particular area in the clinic or classroom, a specific child or client, a team of practitioners?
- There are ethical issues. It may not be appropriate to photograph clients.

Predetermined observational categories
In this case you would use a blank proforma which you had
divided into time intervals (Figure 5.2). In the time column you
would record the moments at which the observation was taken
and consequently any disruptions to the sequence of the observations. In the middle column you would write, usually using a
predetermined set of symbols, what the individual you are
observing is doing at that moment. The third column is left
blank at this stage to allow you to carry out more detailed analysis
at a later date. Here you might look at sequences of behaviour or
interactions.

The predetermined symbols used in the middle column are to
enable you to record quickly what is happening at one moment.
They need to be carefully learnt before starting to observe.
Several practice observations are usually necessary. As this is quite
a tiring procedure it is wise to limit yourself to 10- to 15-minute
time capsules and to make your observations at 60-second
intervals. At the end of each 10- or 15-minute block you can write
other contextual comments on the reverse of the proforma.

The predetermined symbols can be borrowed from existing
research studies. But this should only be the case if you are trying
to replicate that study. Otherwise, ideally, you develop your own
symbols as a result of previous, less tightly structured observations
of behaviours in similar settings.

Danger Points

- Predetermining categories of behaviour can act as blinkers
  which prevent you seeing everything of importance.

Figure 5.2 An observation proforma

- To really pick up the subtleties of behaviour you need a complex category and coding system. This can become cumbersome and difficult to use.

The target method

This has been developed by a number of researchers from the observational methods originally used by Sylva, Roy and Painter (1980) in their study of nursery school children. It differs from the predetermined category system described in two ways. First, it does not use a predetermined recording system, and secondly, it does not demand that you write only what happens at a sampling point of, for example, the 60th second in a minute. Instead you write down the flow of behaviour of your target that occurs over a one-minute interval. It can therefore also provide some frequency data.

The proforma used are similar to those shown in Figure 5.3 but the space for recording behaviours is much larger. You usually find that you can record five or six minutes on an A4 proforma. It is useful to develop your own shorthand. A typical entry for one minute of observing one adolescent who is working with a battery at school might look like Figure 5.3.

The third column is used for coding the behaviours recorded in the second column. The codings will reflect both the behaviours and the research question and will be derived from content analysis (see Chapter 6). In this example it would be possible to arrive at codings which examine the interactions between teacher and pupil and the degree of cognitive challenge or help provided by the teacher. It will also give crude measures of time on and off task.

10.03	TA → 'This's not working'	
−10.04	T dem – talking	
	TA lking @ window	
	T → TA – pting @ bttry	
	TA lks @ bttry	

TA = Target Adolescent   T = Teacher

.**Figure 5.3** An extract from a target observation

Danger Points

- If you don't code the observations *immediately* after making them you will find coding rather difficult.
- Your shorthand in column two may be indecipherable after a few weeks so you may need to fill it out immediately after making the observations.
- It requires some initial practice and it is tiring. You should not attempt more than 15 minutes at a time.

Video taping and audio taping

These are not strictly observational methods. Video taping really does little more than delay the observational procedure. While there may appear enormous advantages to having captured the data on tape there are some danger points.

Audio taping is discussed more fully in Chapter 4. It may be best seen as complementary to some of the time sampling observational methods. It works particularly well alongside the target method as the tape can be transcribed to show the one-minute intervals that correspond to the intervals used in the observations. But again there are danger points.

Danger Points

- Video recordings have a particularly narrow focus and wider contextual data are consequently often omitted.
- Video tapes seduce researchers into over-analysis and consequent uncompleted studies.
- Tape recordings are difficult in natural settings as people move and extraneous noise interferes.

Fieldnotes and analytic memos

These methods form part of a process of analytic enquiry that can be seen as a process of focusing down onto what the key issues to be observed reveal themselves to be. They involve the observer in recording in untimed note format any aspects of a situation that might appear to relate to the research question or field. If, for example, you are concerned with looking at the dynamics at work in an inter-disciplinary work team you would note details of interactions both verbal and non-verbal, evidence of patient or client expectation of team members, lines of communication, status distinguishers in terms of clothing, workspace and other support or any other observable features which might indicate the workings of the team.

Advantages of fieldnotes

• They provide good illustrative data.

• They allow the researcher to ground developing analyses in the realities of the field.

• They pick up the complexities of a situation and include interactions and developments over time.

• They are quite easy to do and writing them after the event provides the opportunity for continuous reflective analysis.

Disadvantages of fieldnotes

• Progressive focusing requires some knowledge of the sociological frames of reference that might be applied to their analyses.

• They provide a lot of data which take time to analyse in a systematic way.

• You need lots of cardboard boxes and an empty spare room in which you can respectively store and analyse the data.

• When finally analysing you can feel that you are groping your way through the data and begin to feel that you are drowning in it.

Fieldnotes are usually made as evidence arises or as soon as possible afterwards. Some researchers keep hand-held tape recorders available and record the information as quickly as possible after the event in that way. Fieldnotes can take a variety of forms but a typical page may be set out rather like the reflective diary outlined in Chapter 4 (Figure 5.4).

As themes and patterns emerge to clarify the research question so the focus of the fieldnotes becomes more defined. Progressive focusing is an important part of the process. Consequently much depends on the quality of the fieldnotes in the early stages and the skill of the researcher in the continuous analytic process.

Date Place Focus	
fieldnotes are written here	patterns and themes that are emerging in the fieldnotes are extracted here

Figure 5.4 Fieldnotes

Competing frames of reference drawn from existing understandings of the field of study are tested against the data and used to shape the analysis. In the example of the inter-disciplinary team study, the power relations, the team and techniques employed for sustaining and challenging existing hegemonic practices would be obvious starting points for the analysis of the fieldnotes. But ideally the analytic frames are only as powerful as the data allow them to be. Should the data indicate that other issues are being played out by the team, new explanatory frameworks would have to be found.

If we return to the onion metaphor, this form of observation–analysis interplay can lead the researcher into attributing meaning to phenomena. For example, access to support staff may have a strong symbolic function within the power dynamics of the work team under observation. The use of that symbol can only be observed when its symbolic function has been noted and its meaning attributed. Consequently the researcher-observer begins to move to issues which lie below the surface of observed behaviour. But these attributions of meaning do have to be soundly grounded and based on the observational data.

Analytic memos are complementary to fieldnotes. The starting point is fieldnote observations and they lead the researcher towards progressively defining the research focus. They usually involve the researcher-analyst in reflective analysis of the field. Complementary to fieldnotes, they operate as a way of recording initial analysis of extensive amounts of fieldnote data. They are usually around two pages in length and contain the key points for reflection on and development of the study. In this way they enable the researcher to keep some kind of control over the boxes of fieldnotes that field methods produce.

Danger Points

- You need to keep the continuous analysis up-to-date.
- You need to be systematic and organise your notes with careful cross-referencing techniques.
- Remember to photocopy your raw data so that you can cut out, colour, sort out your notes in a variety of ways without spoiling them.

Vignettes and critical incidents

Vignettes and critical incidents are essentially a way of presenting fieldnote data. But it is useful to discuss them as methodologies as their use indicates the importance of high-quality fieldnotes and they can serve methodological purposes.

They are short narrative descriptions of people, interactions or situations which can be used to illuminate and develop the reader's understanding of the events under scrutiny. Vignettes are usually descriptive summaries of people and places. Critical incidents are usually summaries of intentions and events.

Should, in our inter-disciplinary team example, the occupational therapist successfully challenge the consultant's interpretation of a client's needs, the strategies used, outcomes and reactions would provide a useful critical incident. Once the incident has been retold several major analytical themes could be explored.

Danger Points

- Critical incidents should represent major themes and should not be colourful but non-representative anecdotes.
- Vignettes equally need to be supported by grounded thematic data. If, for example, you want to describe the consultant as impatient and rigid, you need to be able to justify these descriptions by your analysis of your fieldnotes.

Interviews, focus groups, life histories and other narratives

Most of the methods discussed so far have kept the researcher occupied with the surface layers of the event by focusing on what is happening. Interview and related methods, by contrast, give access to the more complex issues of what is meant by what is happening.

Interviews

Interviews, if well done, allow the voices of participants to be heard and so to direct the analysis and interpretation of events.

Advantages of interviews

- You get a 100 per cent response rate to your questions.
- You can probe and explore meanings and interpretations held by participants.
- You hear the language and concerns of the participant.
- Participants usually enjoy them.
- They yield the good rich data essential to, for example, case study.

Disadvantages of interviews

- Interviews are time-consuming (and costly). A one-hour interview takes at least four hours to type and produces around 30 pages of A4 script.
- They can be an intrusion into the lives of the participants as your probing may go too far.
- The analysis of interview data can be endless.
- Arranging the interviews can become a chore.
- You might be able to get the information you need from a questionnaire.
- They need to be done well.

If, despite these warnings, you decide to proceed with interviews you need to take to heart the claim that interviews need to be done well. While poor questionnaires may nevertheless yield useful data, a poor interview is of little use. We need therefore to look at both how to compile and how to conduct an interview.

Stages in devising an interview

1 Write the research question in the centre of a piece of paper.
2 Brainstorm the question areas onto the paper.
3 Group the brainstormed ideas into themes.
4 Place the themes in order, starting with the least intrusive and ending with the most intrusive.
5 Drawing on the brainstorm, start to write the questions that enable you to explore the main themes – use open-ended questions. 'What', 'When' and 'How' questions are useful. 'Why' questions lead to rational justifications and do not always reveal contradictions and difficulties. 'To what extent' questions are useful but imply a preceding affirmative response. Ask 'real' questions that are driven by your curiosity about participants' lives and perspectives.
6 Put the interview together. Start with factual requests, such as name, age, occupation. Move to non-threatening descriptive questions, for example 'Talk me through a typical day' and then gently on to the more probing questions, for example 'Are there some areas of your work where you feel particularly pleased about what you are doing? What about areas where you'd like to do better?'
7 Always end with a positive question about future plans or a summary of what has gone well so far.

Good conduct in interviewing

1 Arrange sufficient time for the interview. An in-depth interview can easily take an hour. If that is what you need don't politely ask for a few minutes, because that is all you'll get.
2 If you are interviewing busy practitioners think how you can pay them back in some way. Can you take story-time for the infant teacher who has given you her or his lunchtime, give the youth worker a hand in some way, provide some useful reading for the social worker or even offer to help with his or her research project?
3 Find somewhere quiet where you are unlikely to be uninterrupted. Flow and concentration are important in interviews.

4 Almost always tape record the interview. You will not get good quality data unless you do. The short interviews that are used to inform attitude scales need not be tape recorded. But if you intend to analyse the interview you must have it on tape.

5 Sit comfortably and casually on chairs that are of similar height and with no desk or table between you. If you have had some counselling training use it.

6 Assure confidentiality and emphasise the need for detailed and full responses. You are interested in the trivial day-to-day aspects of what is to be said, as here lies meaning and interpretations.

7 Keep a balance between conversational tone and your need to control the direction of the interview. An hour is as long as any interview should last and you need to ensure that your agenda is met in that time.

8 Leave plenty of time for responses after your questions. Reflect back words used by the interviewee. Keep eye contact. Show that you are listening and interested. Refer back to previous responses. Encourage and accept the information you receive. Above all don't be judgemental either positively or negatively. Aim at being sympathetic.

9 Be prepared to switch off the tape and not probe too far if you feel you are causing distress. What you hear may be interesting, but it is an abuse of your own skills unless you are willing to take on a full counselling commitment. Always allow time after the interview for a wind-down.

10 Don't be put off by inconsistencies. These are usually not lies but confusions. Recognise them as interesting and explore them together.

If you are a good and sympathetic listener with a sound memory you'll make a good interviewer. If you are naturally impatient, like to control conversations and are not really interested in finding out how others see the world, then maybe you should consider another method, or at least work on your sympathetic listener skills.

Interviews need not necessarily be individual face-to-face encounters. Telephone interviewing and group interviews can also be part of the researcher's repertoire. Telephone interviewing usually results from questions of feasibility and although it can be very useful, with many of the advantages of face-to-face interviews, it is more difficult to do well and the ethical question of taping a phone conversation has to be cleared.

Group interviews are often advocated as a quick equivalent to individual sessions. Quick they may be, but equivalent they are not. They are almost impossible to tape record and transcribe effectively, impossible to record in note form if you are also running the session, and almost as difficult to record in that way if you are an observer watching the group being led by another. Group effects also come into play as the views of the dominant members are voiced most clearly. Consensus is usually reached and diversity of opinion consequently unrepresented. Nevertheless they can have a part to play in the early stages of a research study when you are still beginning to identify the research question or develop your questionnaires or interview schedules.

Danger Points

- You'll do too many interviews and have more data than you can transcribe and analyse.
- Your interviews will be unfocused and each produce too much information.
- You won't leave enough time for the extensive content analysis often demanded of interviews.
- You'll ignore the warning about taping, simply take notes as you interview and be left with poor quality data and no one left to interview to redeem the study.

Focus groups

These are a form of group interview which are utilised in either the preparatory period of research or to explore issues raised from other forms of data collection (e.g. large survey). Focus groups can add depth to early findings; alternatively, they may support the validation of ideas raised in other methods. Focus groups have gained considerable credibility during the past twenty years through their use in marketing activity and other applied research settings.

Careful attention should be paid to the research question you are exploring and to the establishment of a sample which is representative of the group under attention. Often you can select a voluntary, professional or other group that is pre-existing which could reflect the group that you may wish to examine. Examples might include a local teachers' group, a nursing research group or a voluntary organisation such as MIND for users/carers of mental health services.

Advantages and disadvantages of focus groups largely match those highlighted by Stewart and Shamdasani (1990). Most of the points are similar to those of other group survey activities.

Advantages of focus groups

- Speedy means of gaining information.

- Opportunity to interact directly with respondents.

- Rich amounts of data possible from the open response format and opportunities for interaction between respondents.

- Flexible: opportunities for use in a variety of settings/individuals.

- Results are relatively easy to understand.

Disadvantages of focus groups

- Questions can be raised about the representativeness of the group.

- Results may reflect the strong views/opinions of an individual member of the group.

- Interpretation of open-ended questions may be difficult.

- Directly or indirectly the convenor may bias findings.

Life histories and other narratives

The study of the lives of professionals has become a field of growing interest. At one level if we can understand what makes a good professional we can use that information to inform professional development activities. At another level the very process of revealing one's life history can be a self-informing and personally empowering exercise. Methods used to reveal life histories include extensive but relatively unstructured interviews, journals and individual taped recall. They usually demand that the participants consider and reflect upon developments in their professional lives and contribute in some way to the analytic process. Life histories are often compared so that common patterns or themes may be revealed. These methods are sometimes incorporated in the evaluation systems associated with further professional education so that changes in professional perspective as a result of a course of study can be recorded and discussed.

Other narratives might include self-descriptions written in an essay format, descriptions of a good practitioner, descriptions of an event at work. Like transcribed interviews these produce written texts which are amenable to a variety of forms of analysis and analytic comparison.

Advantages of narratives

- Participants give the evidence in their own voices in their own way.

- Written descriptions can be produced by a large number of people at the same time, for example a class of children.

- They often allow you to examine change over time and across context.

- The story often gives more useful information than simply the sum of its parts.

- Participants often gain a great deal from the self-reflection that accompanies the process.

Disadvantages of narratives

- Life histories can be presented for analysis as a vast amount of rambling data.

- Remembrance can colour the past (but this may itself be usefully revealing).

- There are sometimes confidentiality problems which may prevent the use of the data.

- Participants may find themselves revealing more than they might wish to.

- Analysis of sequential events is difficult to do well.

Life history methods particularly demand strong and trusting relationships with participants which often need to be sustained over time as the life and reflection upon it are slowly revealed. This can make enormous demands on the researcher and may impact on any professional relationship that exists between the practitioner-researcher and participant.

Danger Points

- You won't allow enough time for the gathering of life history data.
- Participants may need your support in some ways after completion of the study.
- You'll have too much data and not be clear about how to use them.

Written information

As we have already stressed, do not under-estimate the usefulness of generally available written information. This can include guidelines for professional practice, children's school work, minutes of meetings, information sheets given to patients, and policy documents. They may be easily collected, but they are often a rich source of information which is amenable to the same forms of analysis that you might apply to interview and narrative texts. Themes and patterns which reveal perhaps a certain coherence, or even incoherence, of thought can be made explicit through content analysis. Similarly, changes in perspectives over time can be easily noted as material is updated and comparisons made.

Danger Points

- You will not appreciate the usefulness of much apparently mundane material.
- You will not be sufficiently systematic in your collection of it.
- There may be confidentiality issues associated with its use in research.

Repertory grid methodology

Repertory grids are the mechanisms used for measuring the relationships between mental constructs or ways of understanding events. They can be used to examine similarities and differences in the ways individuals or groups construe events. They can also be used to examine the relationship between the constructs held by an individual. An example of the former would be a comparative examination of how hospital staff, community staff and clients construe the efficiency of community care. An example of the latter would be an exploration with one teacher of the constructs she or he associates with 'good practice' in teaching.

Personal construct theory (Kelly, 1955; Bannister and Fransella, 1971) provides the grounding for the methodology. The theory has spawned a wealth of literature on its applications in both clinical-therapeutic settings and in research. The versatility or applicability of the theory is mirrored by the creativity applied to the use of repertory grids. All that this chapter can do is to urge you towards the literature and Fransella and Bannister (1977) is a good starting point.

A basic grid enables the researcher to examine the use that an individual makes of the constructs or sets of expectations with which he or she makes sense of the world. The key features of a grid are constructs and elements. The constructs are effectively the bipolar blinkers through which an individual views and anticipates events. For example, we might expect a book to be either boring or stimulating, a person to be either gentle or aggressive. The elements are what is to be construed. They can be people, situations, objects, skills to be acquired, curricular goals, the list is almost endless.

Constructs are labels to which meanings are attached by individuals. Anne might construe each new person she meets as either gentle or hard, preferring the gentle people, seeing them as warm and considerate and interacting with them accordingly. Robin might construe each new person as either hard or weak. He may prefer the hard, dependable person and see the weak as unreliable and at the opposite pole to hard. The personal nature of construct systems does present some difficulties when considering aggregation of responses in a group.

Individual construct elicitation is an important part of the process (see e.g. Fransella and Bannister, 1977). Some research projects may be required to reach this stage only, as lists of constructs and changes in constructs over time might be useful data in themselves. Most researchers are, however, interested in examining the changing *use* of constructs and for this you need to employ repertory grids (Figure 5.5).

CONSTRUCTS[1]

		A	B	C	D	E	F	G
E								
L	A person I admire	3[2]	5	4				
E								
M	A person I find difficult	1	3	2				
E								
N	Me	2	3	4				
T	My ideal self	4	4	5				
S	A good practitioner (name)	3	5	3				

[1] The bipolar constructs might include: A Relaxed – Tense; B Hardworking – Lazy; C Generous – Mean.

[2] In this case a 5-point rating scale has been used in which 5 indicates is very (relaxed) and 1 indicates is very (tense). Ranking systems can also be used in which the elements are ranked on each construct.

Figure 5.5 A repertory grid

There is a range of ways of analysing grids which run from the simple arithmetical to the sophisticated computer programme. Also completed grids can be used as the starting point for in-depth clearly focused interviews. The grids are usually administered on an individual basis and can be used, in appropriate formats, with children as young as four and the learning impaired. Pictures and artefacts can be used as elements.

Some constructs can be supplied rather than elicited. The applications of grids seem almost infinite. But you do need some familiarity with the personal construct psychology literature if you are to avoid over-claiming from your findings.

Advantages of repertory grids

- You can get easily quantifiable data on areas which are usually only amenable to the probings or what are often called qualitative methods.

- They can be applied to a very wide range of issues in creative ways.

- There is rigour and a sound theoretical base underpinning their applications.

Disadvantages of repertory grids

- They are time-consuming to administer as construct elicitation is often an important part of the process.

- Their origins are in a very personal form of psychology. Group constructs are not justified by the underlying theory.

- They were not originally designed as research tools but as therapeutic devices.

Although a relatively simple psychological theory which is presented in common sense terms by Kelly (1955) and by Bannister and Fransella (1971), the psychology of personal constructs and its related methodologies have developed in complexity in the last two decades. This is largely due to its wide applicability. Further reading is therefore essential if this is to be a method you choose.

Danger Points

- You will become so involved in computer analysis you will lose touch with what the data are telling you in quite simple ways. (Usually there is no need at all for practitioner researchers to use sophisticated analysis programmes.)
- You'll get so carried away with the flexibility and opportunities offered by grids that you will produce over-complex grids that will be difficult for participants to work with and for you to analyse.

Existing measures and tests

Almost all the methods discussed so far have required the hard-pressed researcher to start from scratch and compile the data collection instrument. It may therefore seem very tempting to avoid the effort involved and plan a study which requires you to use existing measures, whether they be validated tests of pupils' performances, developmental rating scales or measures of general health and social adaptation.

You may have access to these as part of your professional life. If so there may be ethical limitations in your use of these data in research projects. If the measures are not used in your practice, access to them needs to be assured before you commit yourself to their use in the research agenda you set yourself. Some tests, for example those associated with occupational psychology, operate on a franchise basis and require attendance at training programmes before use is allowed. Others are held by organisations like the National Foundation for Educational Research (NFER) in the UK. The NFER operates a system which restricts access to many of the tests it distributes.

It is also important to check whether the existing assessment devices are actually measuring what you want to measure. Does the test give, for example, scores that reflect only performance in the areas you are scrutinising or are measures in additional variables included in the results produced? You also need to be alert to the effects of context on assessment. Some tests are especially prone to becoming outdated or inappropriate as language use changes with time and culture. How many British children would respond with the word 'pledge' to a picture of a child standing with an arm diagonally across his or her chest in front of the United States flag? Nevertheless, if you are satisfied that the measures available are appropriate they can provide extremely good data.

Being inventive in your methodology

The data collection methods we have presented do not form an exhaustive list of established methods, neither do they do justice to the inventiveness of the hard-pressed researcher. The pragmatic approach to data collection is often the best. One example of research pragmatism was the medical researcher who wanted to gauge the effect of a programme which aimed at reducing the amount of bed wetting occurring in a geriatric hospital. His method was simple. He gained a measure of the average weight of used items of bed linen over one week prior to the implementation of the programme and another average weekly measure of used items of bed linen after the programme had been complete. If the second measure was less per item than the first he could assume that there was less extraneous moisture in the bedding and his programme a success.

Other deceptively simple methods that produce interesting results include interaction tracking in groups. Tracking can reveal quite clearly who dominates, initiates, receives, remains passive or is ignored. Similar interaction patterns can be built up to allow examination of lines of communication in an organisation, friendships amongst children, or a workgroup.

Often the methodology itself becomes the focus of the research study. Some topics present considerable problems for researchers and any attempts at overcoming methodological difficulties can warrant recognition. Ways of getting children to reveal their thinking as they solve problems in mathematics or of accessing the frames of reference of expert practitioners would fall into this category of study.

Your research question leads you, through an examination of design options, to the selection of the data collection method you will use. We have so far emphasised the feasibility aspects of methodology. We therefore need to conclude our introduction to methodology with a reminder that decisions about research questions, design and method have to be made simultaneously so that the implicatations of each for each can be acknowledged at the planning stage. A research question that implies that the voices of participants will be heard probably leads to a case study which includes interviewing as a research method. A question which wishes to explore the impact of a policy on attitudes to practice may require a survey design and an attitude scale.

If the right method does not exist you may need to reconsider your question or you may wish to adapt an existing method to suit your needs. Mindful of the validity and reliability issues raised at the beginning of the chapter, the hard-pressed researcher can become the creative enquirer.

Further reading

The best advanced text available on observation remains Bateman, R. and Gottman, J.M. (1985) *Observing interaction*, Cambridge University Press.

Cohen, L. (1976) *Educational research in classrooms and schools*, Harper & Row, provides a comprehensive guide to research instruments and contains prototypes of the most common ones with details of the processes of analysis. It does appear dated in places but still has much basic detail to offer.

Denzin, N. and Lincoln, Y. (eds) (1994) *Handbook of qualitative research*, Sage, contains chapters on research paradigms, strategies, analyses and interpretation written by key players in the area of qualitative methods.

Margot Ely has put together an interesting and encouraging account of what she describes as the qualitative research work that her students have undertaken: Ely, M. (1991) *Doing qualitative research: circles within circles*, Falmer Press.

Oppenheim, A.N. (1992) *Questionnaire design, interviewing and attitude measurement*, Pinter, is a much welcomed update of Oppenheim's classic 1966 book on attitude measurement. The 1992 text contains a considerable amount of detailed and practical advice.

Personal construct theory has produced shelves of associated texts. Some of these have already been mentioned. Fransella and Thomas (1988) *Experimenting with personal construct psychology*, Routledge, gives a large number of examples of the ways in which repertory grid methods can be used in research in a wide range of professions.

A specialist text on child study is Pellegrini, A. (1991) *Applied child study: a developmental approach*, Lawrence Erlbaum Associates. Pellegrini usefully places his detailed advice on how to conduct research with children in the context of the various theoretical approaches to understanding children's development available to researchers.

Stewart, D. and Shamdasani, P. (1990) *Focus Groups: theory and practice*, Sage, is one of the best textbooks on the use of focus groups. As a step-by-step guide to this technique, it provides a readable and accessible handbook which can be used by researchers across a range of educational, health and other professions. A summarised version of this work by the same authors can be found in 'Focus group research: exploration and discovery', in L. Bickman and D. Rog (eds) (1998) *Handbook of applied social research methods,* Sage.

A more advanced text which focuses on the measurement of social representations is Doise, W., Clemence, A and Lorenzi-Cioldi, F. (1993) *The quantitative analysis of social representations*, Harvester Wheatsheaf.

Chapter 6

Analysis and interpretation of data

Introduction

The collection of data formed the basis of Chapter 5. The purpose of this chapter is to enable you to select an appropriate method of processing that information. The chapter is sub-divided into sections that relate to common means of collecting data. However, you should remember that some analytical techniques may apply to more than one method of data collection. Figure 6.1 presents a flow diagram of research methods and appropriate techniques of analysing data.

To assist you in your analysis of data, the following stages can be identified; not all reports will require you to pay attention to each of these stages:

- identification of appropriate tools that will assist the analysis of your research question (e.g. content analysis, statistical techniques, etc.),
- coding and classification of information,
- use of appropriate descriptive statistics,
- use of statistical analyses to measure association or difference between sets of data,
- interpretation of findings.

A range of the most frequently used methods of data analysis is included within this chapter. You may have embarked upon a project that will involve techniques not covered here (e.g. different statistical tests). Other textbooks exist (e.g. Siegel, 1956) that cover a range of statistical methods. The prime consideration of this

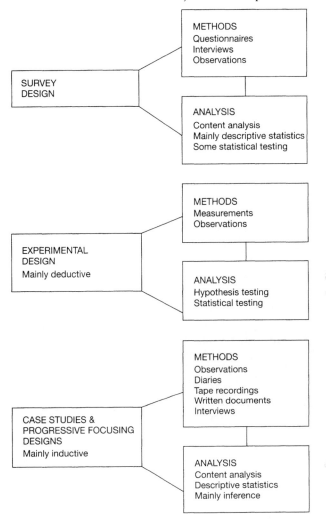

Figure 6.1 Matching design, method and analysis

chapter is to present a range of common techniques rather than the total range of what is available.

Irrespective of the research design and methods utilised, a stage of coding and classification of information must be undertaken. In some cases this will be relatively straightforward; in experimental research definitions of indicator variables (e.g. an age variable or a variable of socio-economic class) should have provided the basis for later analysis. But in many cases, of which survey research and interviews are examples, much initial coding of material must take place. In some studies you may wish to convert qualitative information into quantitative data. For example, in content analysis you may code the presence/absence of certain characteristics, or assess the frequency of certain traits. We shall be looking in some detail at categorisation and coding in the next section.

The first half of this chapter provides details of the analysis of many of the methods covered in Chapter 5. The use of descriptive statistics and of statistical analyses are covered in the latter part of this chapter. Following this chapter you can progress from the first stages of analysis to ways of synthesising information, and, where applicable, testing hypotheses.

Questionnaires and attitude scales

(i) The analysis of questionnaires is usually quite simple. Your original design should have included a final column which could be used for coding purposes. After swift categorisation of data, you can then remove the coding material from the questionnaire sheet and transfer the information quickly to a computer database, for example:

Q10

How often do you attend the Centre?

Daily	Weekly	Other	Coding Column
	/		2

In this case, daily is coded 1, weekly 2, and other 3. You can then proceed to aggregate and compare responses.

(ii) The analysis of open-ended responses in questionnaires will be covered in the later section on content analysis.

(iii) The analysis of attitude scales is more complex. We shall take it step by step.

Step One   Take an unused copy of the scale.

Step Two   Mark all the statements which indicate a negative attitude to the event, for example 'Practitioner research is a waste of time'. You may feel that you will need to reverse the scoring on these at Step Three.

Step Three At the top of the scale give a score to each degree of response. On a five-point scale it would look like this:

	Strongly disagree				Strongly agree
	1	2	3	4	5
'Practitioner research is fun'	_____	_____	_____	_____	_____

Step Four Go through all the responses to each statement in turn, marking the number of responses on each degree of response.

	1	2	3	4	5
'Practitioner research is fun'	I	IIII	II	~~IIII~~ ~~IIII~~	III ~~IIII~~ ~~IIII~~

Step Five Calculate the average response to each statement by multiplying the number of responses on each degree of responses by the score.

'Practitioner research is fun'	1×1	4×2	2×3	10×4	13×5
	1	8	6	40	65

total the item score to   120

and divide by the number of respondents $\dfrac{120}{30}$

The average item score for this item is 4.00 indicating a positive response.

Step Six Other items will score above and below this enabling you to rank order the importance of items.

'Research leads to promotion'   4.12
'Practitioner research is fun'   4.00
'Research helps me plan better'   3.78

> You may want to look at the degree of
> spread of response to some items. A score
> of around 3.00 can be a result of most
> people scoring 2, 3 or 4 or it could be
> due to a wide range of very different
> responses.

Once you have average item scores and can rank order them you
can compare before-and-after intervention results or the attitudes
of different participants (by analysing the groups separately).

(iv) The way you organise and analyse the information from
your questionnaires or scales will depend upon the
questions you are trying to address in your study.

    (a) You may want simple survey level information for
which percentages will be sufficient.

    (b) You may want to rank order overall responses to
an attitude scale.

    (c) You may want to consider the relationship between
responses to some questions and responses to
others, for example differences between recently
trained and experienced practitioners.

    (d) You may want to directly compare responses of two
specific groups, for example practitioners and
managers.

    (e) You may find that after looking at your data there
are relationships you had not previously
considered. This is an exciting element of
research. Do not ignore this, follow it up and
include it in your analysis.

The possible questions you can ask of the data set are considerable and certainly not exhausted by the examples just given.

If you have access to computing facilities, it can help to put the
data set on computer and then run appropriate statistical analyses
on the database. But do not despair if you do not have computing
facilities. There are many advantages to your own mechanical
computations. Above all, doing it yourself allows you to keep in
touch with the data and be alert to possible connections. The
mathematical processes necessary for the types of analysis
suggested in (a) to (d) are all very simple.

Questionnaires lend themselves to the descriptive tabulation
of data, but, on occasions, statistical tests, such as correlation

techniques and chi-squared analysis can be applied. If you are considering the use of such tests, you should refer to later parts of this chapter.

Observational data

The analysis of your observational data will depend upon the purposes of your data collection, your research design and ultimately of course your observational method.

Checklists and event sampling

If you are using prepared checklists or taking counts of events you will produce simple quantifiable data which can be analysed in much the same way as closed question questionnaire data (Figure 6.2). These data are categorical data, of which more will be said later in the chapter.

Time sampling and target methods

Analysis here is more complex and of course much will depend upon the research question. You may be concerned with causal chains of events, that is, what tends to lead to what in an interaction? Or you may be interested in what happens in different situations. An example of this might be the degree of cognitive challenge apparent in children's play when alone, with

Period of observation 30 mins	Teacher A	Teacher B
Initiates interaction with question	10	6
Responds to child's question	17	3
Initiates interaction with request	5	14

Figure 6.2 Semi-analysed event data

	Alone	Peer	Adult
High (minutes)	7	14	13
Low (minutes)	12	5	15

Figure 6.3 Semi-analysed time sample data

peers or with adults present. Your coding systems will need to reflect your research questions. In the cognitive challenge example you will need to determine your definition of high and low challenge (probably drawing on previous research) and classify each interval of observation as high or low and identify the context of the interaction as alone, peer, adult. Eventually, you will be able to present your data in a semi-digested form ready for the application of appropriate statistics (Figure 6.3)

Descriptive observational techniques

In some situations analysis will be incorporated into the process of progressive inferential focusing already discussed in Chapter 5. In others it will be kept simply for illustrative purposes as vignettes. In some cases it may be appropriate to apply one of the forms of content analysis that are outlined in the next section.

Content analysis

Whether you are undertaking survey research using open-ended questions on a questionnaire, gathering interview data, using descriptive observational methods or simply gathering a variety of forms of written material as data, the time will come when you will have to cease these squirrel-like activities and begin to make sense of the material that is accumulating around you. In fact, you will have noted already that we have suggested that it is not in your best interests to wait until you are drowning in data before you start the analytic endeavour. Continuous analysis of data allows you to keep control of the project, to undertake a process of progressive focusing on the most important issues and perhaps to have some responsive reflexivity between your data and the design of the project.

Written text which is ready for analysis can be in the form of interview transcripts, observational jottings, or published (and unpublished) material and documentary evidence. Content analysis of free-flowing text starts by asking specific questions of the text. These questions are, of course, derived from the focus of your research question. Content analysis is based on the assumption that analysis of language in use can reveal meanings, priorities, understandings and ways of organising and seeing the world.

The process of content analysis can be likened to passing a comb through the texts. The comb is shaped by the concerns of the research and the degree of detail required to answer the research questions. Sometimes, like tangled hair, the text fights back, resists the comb and may even alter its shape and hence the research question or concern. An interplay between data and analytic process is therefore an important feature of content analysis.

Just as you can find combs in a variety of shapes, designed for different types of hair and purposes, so there are different degrees of content analysis.

Asking broad questions

If written material is used to provide background material for a more specific analysis of data from another source, it is sometimes sufficient simply to ask some broad questions of the texts.

An example of this would be an observational study of pedagogic practices in several reception classes in infant schools which had as contextual data the written material sent to parents prior to their children's entry to school. Fine-tuned analysis of the observational data would be undertaken, but questions arising from the analysis of the observations could be asked in general terms of the material received by parents. For example, are parents expected to be teachers of their children? Does the school expect parents to respond to all school requests? What kind of requests? Is there a coherent pedagogy evident in the parents' information? What is it? In this example the content analysis of the material for parents is led not by the text-based data being analysed but by questions emanating from elsewhere. In this case it is driven by the analysis of the observational data. It could equally well have been led by broad questions which had their origin in current understandings of pedagogy. Is the advice to parents reflecting a child-centred approach? Is the 'whole child' a concern? What view of the curriculum obtains? Is a sociocultural understanding of teaching and learning evident?

The example we have used indicates that these broad questions are usefully applied to contextual or secondary data. They may also be applied at the start of a process of progressive focusing in which answers to the broad questions allow the research to move systematically towards more specific and detailed analysis of events.

Creating categories and codings

The most commonly used form of content analysis found in practitioner research is more detailed than broad questioning and involves the analyst in combing the data to find themes and patterns or categories of evidence which can then be further broken down and a system of codings applied. Taking interviews with nurses as an example, a theme or pattern which could be called a category in interview data might be derived from the evidence that a number of the nurses interviewed wanted to undertake further study and were motivated to apply for a course to upgrade their qualifications. The category of response could be labelled 'motivated for further qualifications'. But the reasons for wanting to upgrade the qualifications may be various. For example, they might include: 'want a more responsible nursing role', 'need more money', 'want to get out of nursing as soon as possible'. These motivations would be sub-categories of 'motivated for further qualifications' and would be coded to indicate that.

Categories and their sub-categories or codings can emerge from the data and be therefore entirely data-driven. But this is a painstakingly difficult process for hard-pressed practitioner researchers. We will nevertheless briefly explain the process, warn you against it, in its purest form at least, and then suggest a more manageable and valuable alternative.

What we are describing is a form of grounded theory which is derived from the work of Glaser and Strauss (1967). While it has many advantages, not the least of which is the questioning of established ways of categorising the world and allowing the categories of the participants to emerge, it does make considerable demands on the lone researcher and begs the question of the personal theories that any researcher is bound to hold as she or he undertakes a project and starts to notice categories.

Stages in creating data-driven categories

1 Photocopy the text (e.g. an interview).

2 Read through it several times.

3 Identify key sections and number the sections on both copies of the text, for example, Interview 1, Statement 3 = 1.3.

4 Cut out the key sections on one copy, keeping the numbering clear.

5 Sort and group the extracts according to the research focus.

6 Label the groupings and so create your tentative categories.

7 Repeat the exercise with other interviews.

8 Test the robustness of your categories. Do they relate to several interviews?

9 Look for overlap between categories and so firm up category boundaries.

10 Discard weak categories (i.e. that do not appear to relate to many interviewees).

11 Be alert to the need to create new categories and re-sort if necessary.

12 List the category labels and brief descriptions – use a separate page for each category.

Stages in developing codings

1 Take the extracts that comprise a robust category and look for similarities and differences between them.

2 Group the extracts according to their similarities and be prepared to justify the groupings. These now comprise your coding groupings.

3 List each coding grouping under the category label, and descriptor on the prepared page, giving at least one example for each coding.

4 Give a number to each coding grouping.

If you follow this process you will have produced the beginnings of a set of coding instructions for the content analysis of your data. An example of a coding instruction might look like Figure 6.4.

Having created your codings you need to check their validity. You should give several interviews to a willing friend and ask him

Category:

Motivated for further qualifications:

Any evidence of a reason for wishing to upgrade current qualifications should be included here.

Codings:

1 Wants a more responsible role in nursing.
Statements would include reference to lack of challenge in current role; wanting to be able to take on more responsibility as a nurse; wanting more of a team leadership role in nursing.

2 Wants an increased income.
Statements here would focus on promotion as a salary increase.

3 Wants to leave nursing.
Statements here would include the need to get a higher qualification of any kind to escape or to take on an administrative role.

Figure 6.4 Coding instruction

or her to use your coding instructions on the interviews. You would be looking to see whether they can use both your category system and the codings you have applied. You will want to find inter-rater reliability agreement on at least 80 per cent of the data. You may therefore find that the categories or codings will need some modifications as a result of this exercise.

Once you have established the strength of your categories and codings you can use them to sort the full data set. You may wish to present your data simply in terms of themes or categories, using the codings to give illustrative evidence of the sub-categories. Consequently you may be satisfied by simply grouping and storing extracts in coded categories either physically or on disk. Alternatively you may wish to proceed to a more quantitative form of analysis in which the codings are quantified and even made amenable to statistical analysis. This process would involve you in creating a data sheet along the lines of Figure 6.5.

Identifier	Category 1 Wants further qualification	Category 2 Working context is restrictive	Category 3	Category 4	Category 5
$\phi 1$	2	3			
$\phi 2$	1	2			
$\phi 3$	–	1			

Figure 6.5 A content analysis data sheet

In Figure 6.5 Nurse 1 wants further qualifications to increase her salary, Nurse 2 wants a more responsible role in nursing and Nurse 3 did not use that category. With data of these kind available on a data sheet you are able to make a quick quantitative analysis of group perceptions of events, and with your carefully numbered and sorted extracts you can trace back to actual quotations to support the presentation of your analyses with vivid examples of the voices used by participants.

We mentioned earlier in our account of content analysis that the pure data-driven form of content analysis could be replaced by a slightly more easily managed version. As well as being slightly less demanding, the modifications to the process that we shall be suggesting do not beg the question of researcher preconceptions. Instead they simply accept that they are there and evident in the research question itself and in the way the interviews, questions or observational focus were selected.

The more manageable version of content analysis operates with a system of predetermined categories that is derived from, for example, the interview questions or specific foci employed in the observations. While the category construction may be driven by the research instruments, the coding of material grouped under the categories remains data-driven in the way we have already described. Consequently the opportunities for the voices of the participants to be heard are not lessened.

If the cutting and sorting method of data control does not appeal there are alternative ways of dealing with the raw data. The first is equally low-tech and relates particularly to what we have described as predetermined categorisation. To undertake this method of initial data sorting you will need to create proformas that are based on the categories to be examined. Each person interviewed or observed will need a proforma. The proformas should be divided into sections that relate to the interview or observation schedule (Figure 6.6).

In Figure 6.6 the words used by Nurse 3 to explain personal ambitions are rewritten onto the proforma. They can then be coded and represented on a data sheet in the ways already shown. An advantage of this method is that proformas are easier to handle than cuttings.

A more high-tech method involves computer analysis. Content analysis programs are developing apace. They allow easy marking, shifting and sorting of text. It will be worth discussing these with

Name: Nurse 3	Date:	Place:
Interview question 1 Has ambitions?	Interview question 2 Perceived constraints?	Interview question 3 Perceived enablers?
I need better qualifications if I am to increase my job satisfaction. There are times when I get quite bored with ritual and want more challenge.		

Figure 6.6 An initial data sort proforma

your tutor or software supplier as you may find them time-saving and effective.

Simple sorting in on-going analysis

You may well feel that the methods of analysis we have just described are rigorous, but perhaps a little heavy-handed for the data you have. You may simply be looking for ways of sorting and thinking about your findings so that they can raise new questions and take your thinking and practice onwards.

An example of this kind of analysis would be of the tape-recordings made by a teacher of his or her interactions with children on a task. The first stage of the analysis might be to list all teacher questions and children's responses (Figure 6.7).

Teacher questions	Pupils' responses
	(i) = Jane (ii) = Sophie
What is this?	(i) Silence (ii) A battery
How does it work?	(i) Silence (ii) Silence
What happens next?	(i) Silence (ii) You attach that
What do you think might happen?	(i) It'll light (ii) You'll get a buzz sound

Figure 6.7 An initial sorting of data

These data may now be sorted in a variety of ways. These might include

(a)   Questions which got high, medium or low responses.
(b)   Questions which got accurate or inaccurate responses.
(c)   Questions which got expected or unexpected responses.

You may then explore the common features of successful questions or aspects of the surprising responses by further categorisation. You may be able to identify where they are surprising and accurate, or surprising and inaccurate. These simple categorisations can then be considered for their implications for future practice and task setting for pupils.

This kind of data sorting can be entirely pragmatic and creative, addressing itself to the immediate needs of the practitioner and his or her practice, and is most commonly found in the action research process.

Fine-combed analysis

So far we have been asking questions about the data in various ways and have been working on an assumption that selections will be made from the data and not all of it used. However, it may be the case that a fine analysis of, for example, a counselling interaction, a speech, two children on a mathematics task or a discussion between a mother and child is a necessary element in your project.

Careful fine analysis of conversations or behaviour can be fascinating and revealing and for those reasons a little data go a very long way. A ten-minute tape sequence can produce a great deal of information and be time-consuming to analyse. You need to heed any advice that suggests that you should keep your sample small if you are undertaking this form of analysis.

Having collected and transcribed your data your first decision has to be about the unit of analysis. If you are working with a conversation it might appear that a speaker turn or a sentence are appropriate units. But if turns are used you will get no indication of the amount of time one speaker talks compared with another. Also one turn can carry a variety of forms of information, for example, a question, a statement and an attempt at control. If you decide to use sentences you may find it difficult to determine what constitutes a sentence in a conversational flow. An alternative unit of analysis therefore needs to be found. At this point we would like to introduce you to the *meaning chunk.*

These are marked in the following extract of conversation as chunk 1 and 2.

'I enjoy my work [1]/but I find some aspects frustrating at times.'[2]

Each of the two meaning chunks carries a completely meaningful statement and at the same time is a unit of analysis which allows you to see who dominates the discussion, categorise what is said and examine the processes of interaction.

Before starting the analysis of the text it is useful to have in mind a set of at least tentative categories that can apply to the meaning chunks. These categories can be derived from your readings of other research. In the case of a counselling interaction they could be the techniques you would expect a counsellor to use. In a conversation between a mother and a child they could come from other published studies of similar interactions. You will be able to modify and develop the categories as you test them against your data. You will of course need to make your final category scheme explicit when you write up your study.

Stages in fine-tuned analysis

1 Mark and number the meaning chunks in the text (in a conversation you will need to use a numbering system that allows you to identify the speaker).

2 Count the number of chunks and, if appropriate, the individual contributions of each participant.

3 Apply your tentative categories to the meaning chunks. You can either label or list the chunks.

4 Modify or develop new categories if necessary.

5 Record your categorisations of the data in ways which allow you to answer your research questions:
  – you may want to chart how a conversation changes over time;
  – your concern may be the processes of interaction: what triggers what;
  – you may want a simple count or measure of the proportional use of different techniques.

6 Be creative and adventurous in your analysis, for example it may be useful to divide a conversation into time sections so that minute one can be compared with minutes five and ten.

7 Be rigorous and prepared to explain and justify your categorisations.

Content analysis – quantitative or qualitative?

The answer to that question depends upon you and your research question. All the methods of content analysis we have outlined allow us to make some sense of text-based data, whether observational, tape-recorded or printed, without losing the essential qualities of those data, the voices of the participants or the language of the writers. At the same time at least two of the methods allow you to proceed to quantitative analysis of the categorisations or coding produced. If your project demands this, these quantitative analyses are as amenable to statistical description and testing as any other quantitative information. In many ways content analysis gives you the best of both worlds as you can firm up the picture you are presenting by the application of some statistical procedures and yet still paint it vividly by drawing upon illustrative quotations readily available through the careful combing that you have undertaken.

The analysis of case study data

In Chapter 3 we described a case as a unit of analysis and for that reason we need to think specifically about the examination of cases. We also stressed in Chapter 3 the importance of gathering good quality data. A concern with quality is also central to the analysis of case data. Yin suggests that case study researchers should follow four 'principles' (Yin, 1998):

- examine the evidence exhaustively;
- consider 'rival' interpretations of the data derived from other theoretical perspectives;
- focus on the major research questions outlined at the start of the study to demonstrate that you have not simply followed the easy routes through the evidence;
- compare your ways of analysing and your interpretations to as much existing research as possible to show that you are building on earlier work and not reinventing.

These principles apply equally to explanatory, descriptive or exploratory cases (see Chapter 3). We shall now explore Yin's principles as they relate to the case enquiries of practitioner researchers.

Exhaustive examination of the data

Exhaustive examination of data requires you to become even more familiar with the data than you were when you collected them. Familiarisation might involve making summaries, categorising, and playing with various combinations of the data such as field notes and interviews. We are strongly in favour of the idea of being playful with your data throughout the analysis process to allow creative combinations to emerge and to enable you to gain fresh insights. You should give yourself long stretches of uninterrupted time if at all possible while playing with your evidence. The need for rich data, creatively explored in considerable detail, suggests that practitioner researchers undertaking case study work should be modest in their aims. Low quantity and high quality should be the guide for cases if they are to be worthwhile. Importantly, the case study database needs to be well organised so that themes and patterns can be quickly explored and their validity checked. There is no room in case study analysis for logical leaps; instead case study researchers need to be able to tell coherent stories that are supported at every stage by evidence. Our advice on creating categories and codings given earlier in this chapter is particularly relevant here as they allow you to follow trails through your data.

Interpretation of the case data

Interpretation of case data takes us back to our concern with the theorising of the case in Chapter 3. Yin's suggestion is that the interpretation process involves testing not only one's preferred theoretical orientation, but also that of rival theories. For example, if one's aim is explanation, one might interpret a student nurse's growing competence in terms of her acquisition of key skills in practical sessions held on her university course or one might interpret it in terms of her acculturation into the community of practice of a particular ward. In other words, her learning may be being transferred from the university to the ward or it may be heavily situated in the experiences available in the ward. However strongly a researcher may be pledged to the first interpretation, the validity of the second possibility needs to be examined. Other comparative cases therefore need to be scrutinised in the light of the alternative explanations before either explanation becomes the selected interpretation.

Interpretation of case data can present particular problems for practitioner researchers who are close to, or part of, the case being examined. Researcher expertise always informs the interpretation of case data. Indeed researchers who have neither a familiarity with the field of study nor knowledge of wider theoretical interpretations that might be tested in the detail of cases should be advised to avoid case study. Practitioner researchers are almost bound to have at least familiarity with the field of study. But that familiarity can at times blinker us so that we fail to see alternative interpretations of events. We therefore strongly suggest that practitioner researchers do try to achieve some balance between their valuable insider knowledge and the fresh insights that might be offered by a theoretical framing of the events they are studying.

A focus on the major research questions

A focus on the research questions that led originally to selecting case study as a method, can reveal a tension when analysing case data. Case studies do need some theoretical framing but one of their strengths is their capacity to reveal new ways of seeing familiar and complex situations. Too strong an emphasis on one frame and the questions that were derived from it may limit what can be gained from the study (hence the need for examination of rival interpretations). The outcome of the tension between attention to theory and attention to what the evidence from the field is saying is often a richer understanding of both the theoretical framing and the field. This enriched understanding may well include some criticism of the power of the theoretical frame. Yin's point is that we do need to maintain intellectual rigour while analysing the case and should avoid being seduced into simply abandoning theoretical frames that don't appear to fit in order to follow easy pathways through our data.

Of course, evidence that the original framing was misguided may be so overwhelming that one has no choice but to reframe the study. If this happens the reframing becomes part of the story of the study. However, most importantly it will usually require a re-analysis of all the data to ensure that the new frames are generally valid. To return to the nursing competence example outlined earlier in this section: if the original questions were framed in terms of the application of received knowledge rather than the co-construction of knowledge in a community of practice, but the ward data suggests convincingly that the original framing was inappropriate, then other aspects of the data need to be explored in relation to the new framing. For example, the researcher might want to explore links between higher education and the workplace and look afresh at the advice sent to the hospital-based mentors by the university and how the mentors use the advice when working with students.

Reflexivity between design and data is an important element in case study work and requires researchers to see data analysis as an ongoing process. In the student nurse example, once the study had been reframed, the researcher is likely to want to increase the attention paid to the relationships between the student and the more expert colleagues with whom she is working on the ward and so make adjustments to the original design of the study. Yin's advice about attending to the original questions clearly has implications for how those questions are posed. We suggest that case study questions are open questions such as 'how do student nurses learn about providing assistance after cardiac arrests?'. Open questions allow a rethinking of the original theoretical framework while staying on track with the original exploration.

Building on earlier work

Building on earlier work is sound advice for all researchers. But again Yin's advice reveals a tension for case study researchers. Often case study is selected simply because existing work has paid insufficient attention to the perspectives of all the stakeholders in a situation. If, for example, strategies to assist the rehabilitation of heart attack victims are based on the assumption that this is largely a middle-aged male problem, case studies of how women and younger men return to health after an attack may have relatively little previous work to build on. However, case researchers should build on what is already understood and see the analytic process as, in part at least, a conversation between their data, their interpretations and those that have been previously offered by others when looking at similar data.

The advice to build on existing research also returns us to the purpose of the case. It may be entirely appropriate to undertake an explanatory case study as a replication of a case study in another setting. In this way two or more studies can be compared as part of a process of theory building. Exact replication will, of course, be difficult if not impossible. Case studies are messy and very different from research in the controlled conditions of laboratories. However, the complications of replication are themselves revealing. One should therefore not equate replication with reinventing and therefore dismiss it. Equally the analysis of descriptive cases may be illuminated by comparisons with other cases available in the literature.

Summary

In summary, the analysis of case study data aims at offering a coherent and well-substantiated story which weaves together the patterns and themes that have been revealed. It is often helpful to write up the case as it progresses as a case report. You may find that you wish to elaborate later on different aspects of the report for different audiences. But the existence of a coherent report as a working document will assist you wherever you tell the story of the case. At the very least your ongoing case report should include your theoretical starting points and how these develop, your focuses for the study and how your interpretations of these shift, the questions raised by the evidence, and your research design and how that alters in response to other changes.

Statistical analysis

This section should not be seen as a definitive account of this subject. Rather, it acts as a guide to some points that you may wish to reflect upon in developing statistical work for your dissertation or research report. Not all research projects will call for statistical analysis. Some, however, will be meaningless without this element of the research process. Many practitioner researchers wisely use a combination of qualitative and quantitative methods of data collection/analysis. This is to be encouraged. However, if you do choose to do this try to strike a balance between tabulation/explanation and description/evaluation.

In seeking to put together your data, you may wish to reflect upon the difference between *descriptive statistics* (e.g. averages, standard deviations, correlations, and pie charts) and *statistical tests* (i.e. those associated with hypothesis testing).

Descriptive statistics

Many of these measures can be undertaken on a computer with the use of suitable programs (e.g. SPSS-X, Supastat or some spreadsheet programs). The most common descriptive techniques used in survey work or as background information are as follows.

Use of average measures

The term 'average' can include a series of different values. Depending upon the nature of your data, you may find yourself using one or more of the following measures:

* Mode
* Median
* (Arithmetic) Mean

To help explain each of these terms, some short examples are presented. For example, consider the following set of children's ages:

3, 5, 6, 6, 10, 11, 12, 14, 16, 17

The *mode* is the most frequently occurring value. In this case it is 6. The *median* is the middle score of a set of values (when placed in rank order). In this case it is the $\frac{n+1}{2}$th value, which is the 5.5th value, that is 10.5 (midway between 10 and 11).

The (*arithmetic*) mean ($\bar{x}$) or average is calculated by adding together all the values and dividing that result by the number of scores. This can be represented by the formula:

$$\bar{x} = \frac{\Sigma x}{n}$$

In this case it is

$$\bar{x} = \frac{100}{10} = 10$$

There are advantages and disadvantages of using different measures (Figure 6.8).

Graphs of frequency distributions

You might wish to examine the frequency of scores/values. For example, if you are examining the distribution of intelligence – through IQ scores – then the best method to display this material would be through a graph of frequency distribution.

	ADVANTAGES	DISADVANTAGES
Mode	Easy to calculate (where sample is small	Only uses a relatively small amount of the available information
		More difficult to find if data numbers are large (some computer programs do not find it)
Median	Easier to calculate than the mean	Does not use all of the information
	Most suitable when a small number of extreme scores are evident (i.e. when data are not normally distributed)	
Mean	Uses all data	Time-consuming to calculate
		Unsuitable when extreme scores can distort the calculation, i.e. when the data are not normally distributed
		Interval data can only be used

Figure 6.8 Advantages and disadvantages of the mean, median and mode

Assuming a large representative sample, the shape of a frequency graph would be as shown in Figure 6.9.

This accords with the shape of a normal distribution, where:

- mean (the arithmetic average), median (half-way point in the distribution) and mode (highest point in the distribution) occur at the same value;
- it is bell-shaped and has the same shape either side of the mean;

Figure 6.9 Normal distribution curve

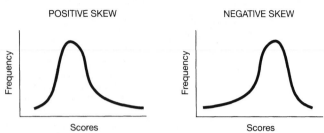

Figure 6.10 Skewed distribution curves

- the curve is relatively flat near the mean, steepens with distance from the mean, and then flattens again further away from the mean;
- it is a perfect normal distribution, there are certain properties of how many values you would expect to find within certain limits around the mean.

However, it is likely that many frequency distributions will be skewed. Unlike the normal distribution, there will be different mean, median and modal values. In skewed distributions the median value will have a higher or lower value than the mode. These will be positive and negative skewed distributions respectively (Figure 6.10).

Skewed distributions may be found where you have a small sample, or a biased sample (e.g. heights of a men's basketball team). In certain cases, where there are zero values that are achievable, you may identify a positive skew or a form of U-shaped curve where the frequency curve declines from an initial peak.

Measures of dispersion
You may find the following to be valuable:

- Range values, including the interquartile range
- Standard deviation

Range values
Two separate values are often used. The ages from the example above will be used.

3, 5, 6, 6, 10, 11, 12, 14, 16, 17

In this example the standard range value is 14 (the difference between the lowest and highest values). Alternatively, some researchers prefer to use the *interquartile range*. This can be calculated from the difference between the lower and upper quartiles.

$$\text{Lower quartile value (LQ)} = \frac{(n + 1)\text{th value}}{4}$$
$$= 2.75\text{th value} = 5.75$$

$$\text{Upper quartile value (UQ)} = \frac{(n + 1)\text{th value} \times 3}{4}$$
$$= 8.25\text{th value} = 14.5$$

$$\text{The interquartile range (IQR)} = \text{UQ} - \text{LQ}$$
$$= 14.5 - 5.75 = 8.75$$

The standard range value rests upon the extreme values at the highest and lowest limits of the distribution. The interquartile range takes into account a greater number of values, and is thus less susceptible to individual extreme values.

Standard deviation
The standard deviation (σ) is a more useful descriptive statistic; it measures the distribution of individual scores around the mean. If the standard deviation is large, then there is much dispersion around the mean; if the deviation value is small, then the degree of dispersion is much less. It is calculated as follows (using the original set of ages):

3, 5, 6, 6, 10, 11, 12, 14, 16, 17

Raw scores (x)	x̄ (mean)	d(x − x̄)	d²
3	10	−7	49
5	10	−5	25
6	10	−4	16
6	10	−4	16
10	10	0	0
11	10	1	1
12	10	2	4
14	10	4	16
16	10	6	36
17	10	7	49

$$\sum d^2 = 212$$
(The sum of d^2)

$$\sigma n - 1 = \sqrt{\frac{\sum d^2}{n-1}} = \sqrt{\frac{212}{10-1}} = \sqrt{23.56} = 4.85$$

There are separate means of calculating standard deviations of a sample and of a population. The larger the sample, the closer the values of each deviation value. At this point you need not worry which of the two standard deviation values you should use; however, you should be aware which measure you are calculating (or that which is calculated by any computer program which you might be using).

Interpretation of a standard deviation can be varied. In isolation, its value is limited. The value of the standard deviation is enhanced when there are several data sets and you are comparing different standard deviations. Amongst samples with similar means but different standard deviations, you could identify which data are more dispersed than others. The smaller the standard deviation, the less the dispersion.

The standard deviation is used in many other statistical tests (especially those associated with parametric statistical tests, see later in this chapter). However, another set of properties concerning standard deviations are found in their uses with normal distributions and standard scores. For normal distributions, approximately 68 per cent of all scores lie within one standard deviation either side of the mean, and approximately 95 per cent within two standard deviations of the mean. This assists you to calculate what proportion of values you would expect to find within certain limits. To help in this process, one of the most useful techniques is that of standard scores, especially z scores.

With these scores you are able to calculate a statistical value which permits you to assess exactly how one individual value compares with any other. For example, in using IQ scores, with a mean of 100 and standard deviation of 15, you are able to calculate a standard score (z score) for any individual. Raw scores (x) of 80 (Person A) and 125 (Person B) can be processed as follows where $\bar{x}$ represents the mean and σ the standard deviation:

$$\text{For 80:} \quad z = \frac{x - \bar{x}}{\sigma} = \frac{80 - 100}{15} = \frac{-20}{15} = -1.33$$

$$\text{For 125:} \quad z = \frac{x - \bar{x}}{\sigma} = \frac{125 - 100}{15} = \frac{25}{15} = 1.67$$

With the use of the table in Appendix A (where z = 1.33 you can ignore the minus sign for this part of the procedure), you will see in the third column that the z score of 1.33 has a value of 0.0918 (i.e. it lies at the 9.18th percentile or 40.82 per cent below the mean value). For the z score of 1.67, the second column has a value of 0.4525 (i.e. it lies at the 95.25th percentile, 45.25 per cent above the mean value).

Such standard scores enable you to compare individual scores on recognised standardised tests (e.g. IQ tests). Alternatively, they are valuable for making comparisons between performances of children on different tests, or of patients on a series of diagnostic tests. For example, a student's high positive z score on maths (compared with a lower score on English) would indicate a relatively better performance in maths compared with English.

Why use the standard deviation?

- Measure of dispersion.

- Used for many statistical tests (e.g. Student's t-test).

- Use with standard scores and standardised tests.

Statistical testing

Within statistical testing there are recognised stages that should be adopted in your analysis. The procedures have their basis in the hypothetical-deductive model identified as part of the background to experimental design. The processes are outlined in Figure 6.11, but will be followed up during the rest of the chapter.

Some tests require data to be in a certain form. Classifications of the different types of data exist (Stevens, 1946, 1951; Upshaw, 1968), but for our purposes, three kinds have been identified for further attention:

- *Interval data.* Interval data are numerical data which come from accepted scales in which regular, measured intervals are recognised (e.g. tests scores, ages, blood pressures, heights and weights). The magnitude of the differences between observations within the data set can be measured. Tests that demand data to be in this format include Student's t-test and Pearson's Product-Moment Correlation Coefficient. You can convert the data to the other two types we now discuss.

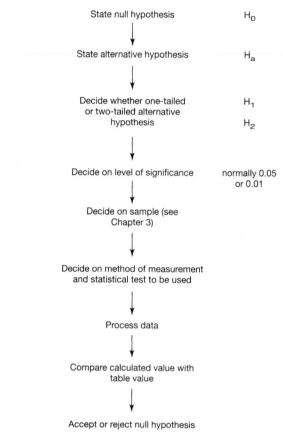

Figure 6.11 Stages in statistical testing

- *Ordinal data.* Data are collected in such a way that they can be put in order or position. An ordinal scale is therefore a set of observations with numbers which indicate which observation had more or less of the underlying property. Examples include the ranking of students' performance on a test. Interval data can be converted to ordinal data by ranking scores, ages and so on. Tests that use ranked data include the Mann–Whitney U test, and the Spearman Rank-Order Correlation. You can convert ordinal data to categorical data (see below), but you are unable to change ordinal data to interval data.
- *Categorical data.* Data are collected or sorted into different categories, such as male/female, or from a questionnaire

survey – yes/no/don't know. Frequencies of each category will be available, and these frequencies can be utilised for the chi-squared test. There is no opportunity for conversion of the data to either ordinal or interval data. The use of the term 'categorical data' is a refinement of the term 'nominal data' used in some textbooks.

Interval data allow you to undertake *parametric* statistical tests, whilst ordinal data and categorical data can only be utilised for *non-parametric statistical tests.*

Parametric statistical tests depend upon your data being normally distributed or having equal variances (technically, the variance is the mean of the squared deviations from the mean). Procedures for assessing whether conditions are suitable for using these tests are presented later in this chapter.

Figure 6.12 is presented to assist you in selecting the appropriate test. Care is needed to:

- consider the characteristics of the data,
- recognise the effectiveness of different tests,
- be aware of any assumptions about background population.

Each test will be examined in turn to give you an idea of the circumstances in which the different tests are used, and to provide a brief explanation of each test. The statistical tests presented in this chapter are a small number of those available for researchers. However, after many years of supervising research projects, it appears to us that these tests form the most common statistical techniques by practitioner researchers in the social sciences.

The need for detail within these sections rests upon the availability of microcomputing facilities. If you have access to a suitable program (e.g. SPSS-X, Supastat) then parts of this chapter relating to manual calculations will be redundant. The program will undertake the computations for you!

Procedures of hypothesis-testing

(a) Formulate hypotheses

As we said in Chapter 3 you have to formulate hypotheses before undertaking experimental research. As part of that process you state a *null* hypothesis. The following statements give examples of null hypotheses:

- The taking of soft drugs makes no significant difference to the taking of hard drugs.
- There is no significant relationship between the amount of fluoride in drinking water and the incidence of tooth decay.

You will often see null hypotheses written as H_0.

It is part of the convention for statistical tests, including correlation, that you state these hypotheses before you begin your data collection and data analysis. Each null hypothesis

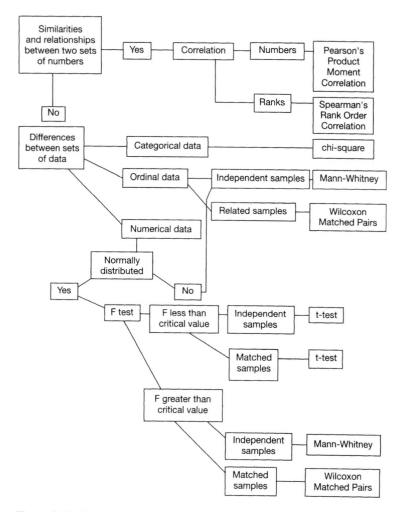

Figure 6.12 Choosing your statistical test

should be followed by an *alternative hypothesis*. There are variations to the specific wording of alternative hypotheses, but appropriate examples for the above null hypotheses might be:

either

- There is a significant relationship between the taking of soft drugs and the taking of hard drugs.
- There is a significant relationship between the amount of fluoride in drinking water and the incidence of tooth decay.

(These are non-directional or two-tailed alternative hypotheses.) You will often see these written as H_2.

or

- Those taking soft drugs are more likely to take hard drugs.
- Increased tooth decay is correlated with low amounts of fluoride in drinking water.

(These are directional or one-tailed hypotheses.) You will often see these written as H_1.

Essentially the decision upon wording of hypotheses remains with yourself as researcher, but it is advisable to discuss them with your tutor. Null hypotheses are unbiased statements, where you are seeking a zero difference or nil relationship between variables/two sets of data. For an alternative hypothesis there is no universal rule, but where possible, try to use a one-tailed/directional statement.

(b) State your level of significance
The next stage is to state your *level of significance*. This is arguably a difficult concept for many, but most researchers are happy to utilise the common levels of significance (0.05 or 5 per cent, and 0.01 or 1 per cent) without worrying too much about the underlying rationale. In brief, the levels of significance refer to cut-off points at which we accept or reject the null hypothesis. Without it we could never reject a hypothesis. For example, a *significant difference* between two sets of data allows you to interpret that there is a large enough difference between the sets of data to reject a null hypothesis that the groups are equal.

When something occurs 5 per cent of the time or less by chance then we can state that the results are not just due to chance. We would reject the null hypothesis; the cut-off point would be the

0.05 significance level (or 5 per cent significance level). Likewise, when something occurs 1 per cent of the time or less by chance then we can state that the results are not just due to chance. We would reject the null hypothesis; the cut-off point would be the 0.01 significance level (or 1 per cent significance level).

The normal convention in most social science and educational research is to use the 0.05 significance level. By using that level of significance you would be rejecting the null hypothesis when the given results would occur by chance 5 per cent of the time or less. Remember, when writing the results and conclusions of the hypothesis, you never prove (or disprove) the null hypothesis – you can only reject or accept that hypothesis at a particular level of significance.

Correlation research

In some textbooks, correlation research forms a research methodology or field of enquiry in its own right (e.g. Kiess and Bloomquist, 1985). Within such textbooks correlational research is presented as a statistical technique in order to assist those researchers undertaking quantitative research where it is necessary to examine relationships between variables.

Many different techniques of correlation exist. However, we shall simply concentrate upon two methods – Pearson's Product-Moment Correlation Coefficient and Spearman's Rank-Order Correlation Coefficient (hereafter described simply as Pearson's and Spearman's respectively). Both techniques are measures of linear association, and they have been designed to produce coefficient values between a maximum (positive) value of +1.0 and a minimum (negative) value of −1.0. A calculated value of +1.0 would display a strong positive correlation. If a scatterplot was produced it would illustrate a linear relationship in which values for one variable increase at a constant rate with the other variable.

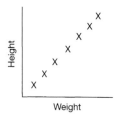

Alternatively, if a calculated value of -1.0 was computed, then it would display a strong negative correlation (see the scatterplot below). This type of relationship displays an inverse relationship in which values for one variable increase whilst values for the other variable decrease.

Statistically, Pearson's is a 'better' test to use, as it takes into account all of the original data, rather than – in the case of the Spearman's coefficient – converting the interval data into ordinal/ranked scores. However, if you are undertaking manual calculations, you will find the Pearson method much more time-consuming than Spearman's. Computer programs will process the information for either method with relative ease (provided, of course, you remember that ordinal data can only be used with the Spearman's method). To help people make their own manual calculations, a case study is presented of the relationship between disposable household income and private health spending per year.

Household	Disposable household income p.a. (in thousands of pounds)	Private health spending (in thousands of pounds)
A	90	0.5
B	45	1.2
C	70	1.0
D	20	0.2
E	25	0.0
F	60	1.4
G	30	0.0
H	35	0.2
I	65	0.6
J	50	1.1
K	110	0.5
L	12	0.0

For the *Pearson* Correlation Coefficient (r) you will need to use the following formula (with disposable household income being variable x and private health spending variable y):

$$r = \frac{n \sum xy - \sum x \sum y}{\sqrt{\{(n \sum x^2 - [\sum x]^2)(n \sum y^2 - [\sum y]^2)\}}}$$

where n = no of households and $\sum$ = summation symbol.

x	y	xy	x^2	y^2
90	0.5	45	8100	0.25
45	1.2	54	2025	1.44
70	1.0	70	4900	1.00
20	0.2	4	400	0.04
25	0.0	0	625	0.00
60	1.4	84	3600	1.96
30	0.0	0	900	0.00
35	0.2	7	1225	0.04
65	0.6	39	4225	0.36
50	1.1	55	2500	1.21
110	0.5	55	12100	0.25
12	0.0	0	144	0.00

$\sum x = 612$ $\sum y = 6.7$ $\sum xy = 413$ $\sum x^2 = 40744$ $\sum y^2 = 6.55$

Thus

$$r = \frac{12 \times 413 - 612 \times 6.7}{\sqrt{\{(12 \times 40744 - 612^2)(12 \times 6.55 - 6.7^2)\}}}$$

$$= \frac{855.6}{1963.64} = 0.44$$

At the 0.05 significance level, the tabulated value is 0.5760 (Appendix B). Since the calculated Pearson's correlation coefficient is *less* than the table value the correlation is a weak one, and is *not* significant.

For the *Spearman* method, the data are converted to ranks before use of the following formula:

$$r_s = 1 - \frac{6 \sum d^2}{n^3 - n}$$

Thus, using the same data regarding disposable household income and private health spending:

Household	Disposable household income p.a. (in thousands of pounds)		Private health spending (in thousands of pounds/ household)		Differences between ranks of x and y	
	x	Rank of x	y	Rank of y	d	d^2
A	90	2	0.5	6.5	4.5	20.25
B	45	7	1.2	2.0	5.0	25.00
C	70	3	1.0	4.0	1.0	1.00
D	20	11	0.2	8.5	2.5	6.25
E	25	10	0.0	11.0	1.0	1.00
F	60	5	1.4	1.0	4.0	16.00
G	30	9	0.0	11.0	2.0	4.00
H	35	8	0.2	8.5	0.5	0.25
I	65	4	0.6	5.0	1.0	1.00
J	50	6	1.1	3.0	3.0	9.00
K	110	1	0.5	6.5	5.5	30.25
L	12	12	0.0	11.0	1.0	1.00
					31.0	115.00

$$r_s = 1 - \frac{6 \times 115}{12^3 - 12} = 1 - \frac{690}{1716} = 1 - 0.40 = +0.60$$

Thus, at the 0.05 significance level, the tabulated value for when n = 12 is 0.506 (Appendix C). You can reject the null hypothesis that there is no significant correlation between the two variables. You would identify the significant positive correlation between disposable household income and private health spending.

It is of interest to note that different conclusions have been identified for the same data utilising the two correlation techniques. Either technique could be used with the original interval data. In some circumstances it is more appropriate to use one technique rather than the other. Whilst we did not test for whether the data were normally distributed, the spread of data did not appear to rule out use of the Pearson method. Arguably, with some extreme values for household income (e.g. 110, 90 and 12) there is an argument in favour of use of the Spearman method (which, by using rank data, is not concerned with such values). However, irrespective of the method used, the important feature in any research report is the interpretation of the results of the analysis.

Both Pearson's and Spearman's are techniques of linear correlation. Other texts (e.g. Burroughs, 1975) give a more detailed account of other correlation techniques, including partial correlation. However, those students who have sets of inter-related variables may wish to utilise techniques of multivariate analysis such as factor analysis or cluster analysis where vectors or groupings respectively of similar variables are identified. These may be beyond the scope of most undergraduate reports, but they

---

Advantages of correlation techniques

- Examine the relationship between variables.

- Appropriate for study of 'real-life' settings.

- Useful exploratory techniques for large or small samples.

- Relatively easy to calculate (especially Spearman's).

- Can be used for interval and ordinal data.

Problems with the use of correlation techniques

- Descriptive, rather than explanatory methods of analysis (i.e. they are *not* measures of causation).

- Unsuitable for use with very small samples.

- Danger of superficiality. Correlations could mask a complex set of relationships.

- Ease of calculation could lead to a large number of correlation coefficients that have no identifiable interest.

- Care is needed to select the most appropriate technique (not all correlation techniques are suitable in every circumstance).

---

are worth consideration when conditions are appropriate.

Chi-squared test (often written as the χ^2 test)

This statistical test is used on categorical data, where frequencies of different categories are identified. Each category must be independent from one another (e.g. male/female; different age categories; different social classes). The χ^2 test is used to investigate whether the observed results (O) are significantly in agreement with or are significantly different from the results which would have been expected (E). χ^2 is a measure of the deviation of the 'O' results from the 'E' results. The formula is:

$$\chi^2 = \sum \frac{(O - E)^2}{E}$$

| | | Different groups of workers | | |
		Health workers	Other workers	Unemployed	Row total
		A	B	C	
Awareness of campaign and active in implementation	i	//////// /////	/////// ////	///// //	31
Awareness of campaign, but not implementing	ii	/////// /////	/////// //////	//////// //	35
Non-awareness and no implementation	iii	//////	///////	//////// ////	25
Column total & grand total		31	31	29	91

At an early stage you will need to place your data in a table consisting of separate boxes. For example, if you have been examining awareness of healthy eating campaigns amongst different groups of workers, you will need to design a suitable table. An example is given, together with the initial analysis of data; please note, you need to be clear in your differentiation between different categories – the test relies upon independent categories. Data can be compiled from responses to questionnaires, interviews and other sources.

Before the analysis is carried out you must write down a *null* hypothesis: there is no significant relationship between occupation and awareness and implementation of a healthy eating campaign. An *alternative* hypothesis would be that there is a significant relationship between occupation and awareness and implementation of a healthy eating campaign. In such circumstances the normal significance level would be 0.05.

The next stage of the analysis is to compare the observed and expected values. This can be time-consuming, and computer programs can undertake this exercise very speedily for you. For each category you can find the expected value as follows:

$$\frac{\text{row total} \times \text{column total}}{\text{grand total}} = \text{expected value}$$

For the top-left box in the above table (Ai) the expected value would be:

$$\frac{31 \times 31}{91} = 10.56$$

In the next table each expected and observed value is presented (observed values are in parentheses).

	A	B	C
i	10.56 (13)	10.56 (11)	9.88 (7)
ii	11.92 (12)	11.92 (13)	11.15 (10)
iii	8.52 (6)	8.52 (7)	7.97 (12)

To calculate the χ^2 test statistic you will need to work out contributing values for each of the nine categories of the table. Thus, for category Ai, the value would be:

$$\frac{(O - E)^2}{E} = \frac{(13 - 10.56)^2}{10.56} = 0.56$$

For the sum of all of these categories, the χ^2 test statistic is as follows:

$$\chi^2 = 0.56 + 0.02 + 0.84 + 0 + 0.10 + 0.12 + 0.75 + 0.27$$
$$+ 2.04 = 4.70$$

The calculated χ^2 value is then compared with a tabulated value (see Appendix D when the significance level is 0.05). The degrees of freedom (df) equates to the number of rows less one multiplied by the number of columns less one (in this case, $2 \times 2 = 4$). The table value is 9.49, and the calculated value falls below that value. In this situation, you cannot reject the null hypothesis; thus you can conclude that – on the evidence presented here – there is no significant relationship between occupation and awareness and implementation of a healthy eating campaign.

Small samples cannot be used with the χ^2 test. In addition, when there are only four categories, the Yates Correction Factor should be used (most computer programs will do this automatically). The formula is amended as follows:

$$\chi^2 = \sum \frac{([O - E] - \frac{1}{2})^2}{E}$$

[O − E] means that you calculate the difference between O and E and ignore whether the result of O and E is positive or negative.

The χ^2 test cannot be used if expected frequencies are calculated at less than five in 20 per cent or more of the categories. Furthermore, no expected frequency should be less than one. Such conditions for the test's use can be stringent, and thus the small-scale researcher has to be wary about expecting to use this technique when conditions may not be appropriate. Having presented some problems, it is worth mentioning that it can be a salvation for many survey reports (provided there is sufficient sample size to give valid results). It is the most appropriate technique to use with categorical data.

Advantages of the χ^2 test

- Used for categorical data (other data can be converted to this).

- Allows a study of relationships/differences between data.

- It is relatively easy to code data for subsequent analysis.

Problems with use of the χ^2 test

- Care is needed in interpretation, especially if you have large numbers of rows and/or columns.

- Is the correction factor required?

- Largely descriptive measure, but can highlight good ideas for further exploration.

- No expected frequency in any category should be less than one; and expected frequencies should not be less than five in 20 per cent or more of the categories.

- Cannot be used with small samples. There is no absolute rule about sample size, but even with a 2 × 2 categorical table, there would have to be a sample size of at least 20. Higher sample sizes are recommended; this is imperative as the number of columns and rows increase.

Non-parametric statistical tests (Mann–Whitney and Wilcoxon tests)

Data are used for these tests in an ordinal format – there is no need to have interval measurements (grades, for instance, could be used). In many cases, interval data are converted to ordinal form. Non-parametric tests are commonly employed – often as an alternative to Student's t-tests – when the measurements fail to achieve interval scaling or where the researcher cannot justify the assumptions about parametric tests. Two of the non-parametric tests most commonly used are as follows:

The Mann–Whitney U test

This test calculates a test statistic 'U', that helps you determine whether a programme or treatment has produced a significant difference between the performances of two samples on some measure. It focuses on the rank ordering of cases and checks to see if there is a statistically significant difference between the ranking of one group's members as compared with another group on the same measure. It answers the question 'Is there a statistically significant difference between the two groups as displayed by the average ranks (or positions) of their members?'

$$\text{Test statistic U} = n_1 n_2 + \frac{n_1(n_1 + 1)}{2} - R_1$$

where n_1 = the number in sample 1

n_2 = the number in sample 2

R_1 = the sum of the ranks (positions) of group 1

The tables provided allow you to determine the *critical values of U.* If the values of U calculated are less than or more than the critical values from the table then the null hypothesis can be rejected.

Reject H_0	Accept H_0	Reject H_0
Lower Critical Value	Higher Critical Value	

Example

You are testing the effectiveness of a new reading scheme (with 'experimental' and 'control' groups).

H_0: There is no significant difference in the reading scores of the two groups.

H_1: Use of the new reading scheme produces significantly higher reading scores.

(one-tailed test) Significance level = 0.05

The results are as follows:

Sample 1 ('Experimental')	Sample 2 ('Control')
140	130
147	135
153	138
160	144
165	148
170	155
171	168
193	
n = 8	n = 7

First rank the groups

	C	C	C	E	C	E	C	E	C	E	E	C	E	E	E
Position	130	135	138	140	144	147	148	153	155	160	165	168	170	171	193
Rank	1	2	3	4	5	6	7	8	9	10	11	12	13	14	15

Sum of rank of group $1 = R_1$

$$= 4 + 6 + 8 + 10 + 11 + 13 + 14 + 15 = 81$$

$$U = n_1 n_2 + \frac{n_1(n_1 + 1)}{2} - R_1$$

$$= 8 \times 7 + \frac{8(8 + 1)}{2} - 81$$

$$= 56 + 36 - 81$$

$$= 11$$

Using the tables (Appendix E) for a one-tailed test with a significance level of 0.05 the critical values of U can be seen to be 13 and 43.

Reject H_0	Accept H_0	Reject H_0

11 13   43
(U)

The value of U lies outside the region whereby the null hypothesis would be accepted. Therefore you can reject the null hypothesis and accept the alternative hypothesis that use of the new reading scheme produced significantly higher reading scores.

Advantages of the Mann–Whitney U test

• Tests differences between sets of data.

• Is non-parametric, thus is suitable for circumstances when parametric tests are not possible.

• Relatively straightforward to calculate.

• Can be used with small sample sizes.

Problems with use of the Mann–Whitney U Test

• Test is not as efficient as the t-test.

• With large samples, procedures should be undertaken to see if parametric tests can be used.

The Wilcoxon Matched Pairs test

This test is suitable for those situations when you are comparing two samples which are matched in pairs (often the samples will consist of the same group of people or subjects before and after some process, in order that you can observe them at two points in time and treat the scores as a pair of results). Data utilised can be interval or ordinal, but in either case the actual difference must be calculated either manually or by the computer. In order that the result is valid, the magnitude of the differences between scores, grades or values must be defended or open to scrutiny. Two differences between scores on a personality scale (e.g. between 1 and 5, and between 3 and 7, on a ten-point scale) or between grades (e.g. between A and C, and between B and D) must represent variations of similar dimension. If these differences vary then another statistical test must be used (e.g. sign test), but they lie outside the remit of this textbook. You may wish to consult the work of Siegel (1956) which will indicate the appropriate non-parametric test to use in the circumstances in which you find yourself.

The Wilcoxon test examines the performance of one group against the other by looking at the difference for each pair between the performance of one subject in the first group and the performance of the matched subject in the second group. If there is no difference between the samples (null hypothesis, H_0) then on average you would expect the first sample to outscore the second group as often as the second sample outscored those of the first. As the groups begin to show a marked difference this will show up by one sample scoring consistently better.

The test statistic T allows you to state whether the imbalance of performance of the two samples is sufficiently large for you to state whether there is a significant difference between the two groups.

Example

Suppose you are conducting a leadership experiment. You have matched individuals across two groups on intelligence. You establish two groups (group 1 'experimental' and group 2 'control'). Group 1 undertake a leadership training course, and at the end of that course, independent observers rate the leadership qualities of each subject on a 50-point scale.

Matched pair	Scores for leadership	
	Group 1 ('experimental')	Group 2 ('control')
A	46	39
B	45	40
C	36	42
D	39	26
E	30	29
F	26	30
G	26	17
H	23	20
I	18	12
J	17	9
K	16	18
L	16	10
M	14	14

H_0 (null hypothesis): There is no significant difference in the scores of the experimental and control groups.

H_1 (one-tailed, alternative hypothesis): Significantly higher scores have been achieved by those attending a leadership course.

Significance level = 0.05.

Next you need to determine the difference between the scores for each matched pair. You need to be consistent in taking one column of scores from the other (e.g. the control column score from the experimental column score), as the direction of the differences can be very important.

Matched pair	Scores for leadership		Difference
	Group 1 ('experimental')	Group 2 ('control')	
A	46	39	+7
B	45	40	+5
C	36	42	−6
D	39	26	+13
E	30	29	+1
F	26	30	−4
G	26	17	+9
H	23	20	+3

(cont.)	Scores for leadership		Difference
Matched pair	Group 1 ('experimental')	Group 2 ('control')	
I	18	12	+6
J	17	9	+8
K	16	18	−2
L	16	10	+6
M	14	14	0

(We can discard M, where there is no difference)

We put differences in order *ignoring the signs* and assign ranks (positions)

	E	K	H	F	B	C	I	L	A	J	G	D
Difference	1	2	3	4	5	6	6	6	7	8	9	13
Rank	1	2	3	4	5	7	7	7	9	10	11	12

Where there are ties the average position is given. For example, in the cases of matched pairs C, I and L, they cover the ranks, 6, 7 and 8. The average value is therefore 7.

The table is completed as follows (ranks associated with negative differences are circled):

Matched pair	Scores for leadership		Difference	Rank of difference
	Group 1 ('experimental')	Group 2 ('control')		
A	46	39	+7	9
B	45	40	+5	5
C	36	42	−6	⑦
D	39	26	+13	12
E	30	29	+1	1
F	26	30	−4	④
G	26	17	+9	11
H	23	20	+3	3
I	18	12	+6	7
J	17	9	+8	10
K	16	18	−2	②
L	16	10	+6	7
M	14	14	0	−

The ranks of the positive and negative differences are added separately.

Ranks of those with negative differences:

$$7 + 4 + 2 = 13$$

Ranks of those with positive differences:

$$9 + 5 + 12 + 1 + 11 + 3 + 7 + 10 + 7 = 65$$

The Wilcoxon test statistic (T) is that which gives the smaller of these two sums (13). This value is then compared with a critical value obtained from Appendix F. In that table, when there are 12 pairs (N), a one-tail test and significance level of 0.05, the critical value of T is 17. If your value of T is *equal to or less than* the critical value, you reject the null hypothesis. In rejecting that hypothesis, you accept the alternative that leadership training does makes a difference.

Advantages of the Wilcoxon Matched Pairs test

- Tests matched pairs data.

- Tests improvement or variation in performance over time.

- Non-parametric, thus suitable for circumstances when parametric tests are not possible.

- Relatively straightforward to calculate.

- Can be used with sample sizes as low as six.

Problems with use of the Wilcoxon Matched Pairs test

- Test is not as efficient as the t-test.

- Data needs to be numerical so that differences can be calculated.

- With large samples, procedures should be undertaken to see if parametric tests can be used.

Parametric statistical tests (the t-test)

(a) Testing for differences in interval data

If you are using interval data and wish to test for differences between two sets of data, then you should see if it is possible to use the t-test. This is the most powerful of all statistical tests highlighted in this handbook. However, for it to be calculated, the conditions must be suitable for use of a parametric statistical test. As a guide to whether conditions are suitable, two criteria should be borne in mind:

- Do the data scores approximate to a normal distribution?
- Do the sets of data have similar variances?

In the first case this may be done by eye; does the scatterplot have a similarity to the normal distribution? Do most of the values fall near the mean of the data? Or is the spread of values such that a very different shape of the data is revealed? For example, are most of the values at either end of the scatterplot (e.g. in the case of percentages, are most of the values between 0–10 and 90–100 per cent with very few values lying between these extremes?). In these cases, it would not be appropriate to use the t-test; instead, non-parametric statistical tests should be used.

For the second criteria, the F-test is used to determine whether the variances of the two sets of data differ statistically from one another. The variance is the square of the standard deviation. Again, many computer programs will calculate the F value for you. If not, the equation is as follows:

$$F = \frac{(\text{standard deviation of sample with larger standard deviation})^2}{(\text{standard deviation of sample with smaller standard deviation})^2}$$

Example
A teacher wishes to determine whether a new teaching method has any effect upon the scores of children. The results for experimental and control groups are as follows:

Experimental	12	14	10	8	16	5	3	9	11	
Control		21	18	14	20	11	19	8	12	13	15

Are the variances similar, and can the t-test be used?

Standard deviation of experimental group = 4.12
Standard deviation of control group   = 4.28

$$F(\text{calc}) = \frac{(4.28)^2}{(4.12)^2} = \frac{18.32}{16.97} = 1.08$$

Degrees of freedom (df) of a sample = Number in sample − 1

Experimental group = 9 − 1 = 8 (smaller SD sample)
Control group = 10 − 1 = 9 (larger SD sample)
df = 8/9

Referring to Appendix G, please note that the top line α (significance level) = 0.05 and bottom line in each horizontal row $\alpha = 0.01$.

Find the column corresponding to 9 along the top of the table and run down this column to the horizontal row corresponding to 8.

F ratio (i.e. F table) = 3.39 at $\alpha = 0.05$

Our value of F (calc) (1.08) was less than 3.39 therefore we can conclude that the variances are similar. We can therefore proceed to use of the t-test.

(b) Testing for significant differences in samples

The t-test is used to examine whether two samples differ significantly from one another. It is presumed that you remember the general points about hypothesis testing (null hypothesis and alternative hypothesis), the direction of the hypothesis (one-tailed or two-tailed?) and significance levels.

The method of the t-test depends upon the nature of the data; there are separate methods for non-paired and paired scores. In the former case, the two samples are independent of one another, whilst in the latter the data can be matched together for each individual/object.

The t-test is one of the most powerful statistical tests available to the practitioner researcher. Its value surpasses that of the non-parametric tests. However, it can be time-consuming in its calculation if no statistical program is available.

The formula for independent samples is as follows:

$$t = \frac{\bar{x}_1 - \bar{x}_2}{\sqrt{\dfrac{N_1\sigma_1^2 + N_2\sigma_2^2}{N_1 + N_2 - 2} \times \dfrac{N_1 + N_2}{N_1 N_2}}}$$

where $\bar{x}_1$ = mean of sample one

$\bar{x}_2$ = mean of sample two

N_1 = number in sample one

N_2 = number in sample two

σ_1 = standard deviation of sample one

σ_2 = standard deviation of sample two

In the following example, you can see how the t-test can be calculated manually (means and standard deviations have been prepared already).

Example
30 pupils were admitted to a school and given a standard test which showed a mean score of 47 points with a standard deviation of 8 points. At the end of the year 25 pupils were left in the class and a similar list showed a mean of 52 points and a standard deviation of 10 points. Had there been any improvement over the year?

> H_0: there is no significant improvement in the
> performance of pupils over the school year
> H_1: there is a significant improvement in the performance
> of pupils over the school year
> Significance level $(\alpha) = 0.05$
> Direction of hypothesis = one-tailed

Here is the calculation (please note that x_1 and x_2 have been reversed; in our calculation we are concerned only with differences between the means).

$$t = \frac{52 - 47}{\sqrt{\frac{30 \times 64 + 25 \times 100}{53} \times \frac{55}{30 \times 25}}} = \frac{5}{2.47} = 2.02$$

A table value of 1.67 is identified from Appendix H. You need to remember that you have a significance of 0.05 *and* a one-tail test. This is important when you examine the Appendix. For the degrees of freedom you sum together the numbers in each group (minus two) which is 53 degrees of freedom. The nearest table value is at 60 degrees of freedom (this is as close as we can go), a value of 1.67.

For the null hypothesis to be rejected, t (calculated) must be greater than the critical value found in the t-table. In our example, the calculated t-value (2.02) was greater than the table value (1.67); therefore we reject the null hypothesis. In conclusion, we can say with some assurance that there has been a significant improvement in the performance of pupils over the school year.

(c) Testing with paired scores

A different procedure is followed when you have paired scores. The formula is as follows:

$$t = \frac{\bar{x}}{\sigma_x} \sqrt{N - 1}$$

where $\bar{x}$ = mean of the gains

σ = standard deviation of the gains

Example

10 children are given a new instructional method in arithmetic. Results showed the following:

Child	a	b	c	d	e	f	g	h	i	j
BEFORE	6	4	3	5	7	2	4	3	5	6
AFTER	7	5	8	7	7	4	3	4	7	7
GAINS	1	1	5	2	0	2	−1	1	2	1

H_0: there is no significant improvement in the performance of the children

H_1: there is a significant improvement in the performance of the children

Significance level (α) = 0.05

Direction of test = one-tailed

So, is there any evidence of improvement in the ability of the group?

Mean = 1.40

Standard deviation = 1.58

N = 10

The calculation is as follows:

$$t = \frac{1.40}{1.59} \times \sqrt{9} = 2.66$$

with 9 degrees of freedom (i.e. df = N − 1)

Again, when comparing this calculated value of 2.66 with the table value of 1.83 (Appendix H) we reject the null hypothesis. Evidence suggests that there is a significant improvement in the children's performance.

Advantages of using t-tests

- Most powerful statistical test.

- Parametric tests utilise all of the data, through use of the mean and standard deviation.

Problems with the use of t-tests

- Conditions must be met.

- Can be time-consuming to calculate by hand.

- For use only with numerical data.

- Danger of inferring too much from a statistical process. Need for the results of the test to be explored in the context of the research.

Summary

In concluding this chapter about data analysis, remember that this part of your research is not just about data handling. It leads you to think about interpretation of the data being analysed. It might be worth remembering the following questions:

- What have I been asking?
- What did I find?
- If I have used hypotheses, have they been supported or rejected?
- Are findings clear?
- What implications are there from these results?

If you are happy with the clarity of your responses to these questions, then you are almost through some of the most time-consuming parts of your project.

Further reading

Glaser, B. and Strauss, A. (1967) *The discovery of grounded theory*, Aldine. This is the starting point for an understanding of content analysis.

Krippendorff, K. (1980) *Content analysis: an introduction to its methodology*, Sage. A helpful basic text on content analysis.

Bickman, L. and Rog, J. (eds) (1998) *Handbook of applied social research methods*, Sage. This is an excellent collection of papers from researchers working in the fields of health, medicine, education, management etc. in the US. It contains a particularly useful paper by Robert Yin on the analysis of case study data.

Heyes, S., Hardy, M., Humphreys, P. and Rookes, P. (1986) *Starting statistics in psychology and education: a student handbook*, Weidenfield & Nicolson. For many researchers undertaking their first dissertation there may be a need to consult a very basic text in the use of statistical techniques. Many such books exist; this book is ideal for the lay person seeking explanation of initial methods of analysis.

Kinnear, R. and Gray, C. (1994) *SPSS for Windows made simple*, Lawrence Earlbaum, lives up to its title by combining an introduction to SPSS with useful advice on the selection of statistics.

Robson, C. (1994) *Experiment, design and statistics in psychology*, Penguin, is a clearly written yet comprehensive introductory text.

Siegel, S. (1956) *Nonparametric statistics for the behavioural sciences*, McGraw-Hill. As you become more proficient in the use of statistical techniques you may find that you require a more detailed textbook. Siegel's work is a classic in the use of non-parametric tests.

Chapter 7

Writing up

What kind of report?

It is at this point that many practitioner-researchers have to confront a dilemma that may have quietly dogged them throughout all the previous stages of the enquiry. Some employers are willing to sponsor the research activities of staff because they believe that the outcomes of the research will generally benefit practice. We would not wish to quarrel with this premise. But problems do seem to arise when the outcome is perceived as a report which can inform local policy. It is highly unlikely that the research dissertation will be able to double as an internal or public report. Matters of confidentiality and the demands of the format and style of a research dissertation usually necessitate the preparation of separate presentations: one a dissertation, the other a report. With that distinction in mind we shall concentrate in this chapter on writing a dissertation, but shall briefly examine other ways of reporting research-based information.

What goes where?

The relationship between form and content in a dissertation or thesis is marked. There are several basic formats. Each is directly related to the type of research question asked and the consequent research design. For example, experimental or survey-based studies will require clear tabular presentation of several elements of the results that have been obtained before moving the reader on to an analysis which examines relationships between these results. Action research, on the contrary, demands a continuous interplay between what is found out, analytic reflection on findings and the design of the next action. It would therefore be impossible to present an action research study within the constrained format which is appropriately applied to a piece of experimental or survey research. The constraints applied to the survey study ensure that analysis rather than description occurs. The freedom given to an action research study allows for an interplay between reflection and action.

Whichever format best suits the focus and structure of your study there are some key attributes which every piece of formally presented research should have.

- Readability: so that it can be clearly and quickly understood.
- Clear organisation: so that the reader is easily led through the text.
- A logical reference system: so that the reader can quickly follow up a reference you have used.
- Information presented in a logical order: so that the reader does not at any point have to guess at, for example, how you analysed your data or reached a conclusion.
- Substantiation: so that each claim can be seen to be based on evidence.

A keyword summary of these points reads

CLARITY	LOGICAL STRUCTURE	EVIDENCE

We will look in turn at three basic dissertation formats: the traditional empirical study, the progressive enquiry, and action research. Each format is presented as a type, not as a pre-scription. While we would urge you to ensure that all the elements mentioned are included in your final presentation, with the support of your tutor you should be able to break or bend the rules so that your ideas and data are presented to best advantage.

Every dissertation needs to open with an abstract and table of contents and end with a bibliography and possibly appendices. We will look at these universal features after examining the three presentation options.

The traditional empirical study

Despite its rather soulless label this is a model that is amenable to a wide range of uses. Some case study work, for example, fits easily into this mode of presentation. It has simple logic to its structure and is often considered to be the easiest framework to use as the constraints it provides do, very firmly, structure how the study is presented. The percentage of total wordage shown gives some indication of the relative weightings of chapters.

Chapter 1 – Introduction (10%)

Central to this chapter is a statement about the research question or hypothesis. This is contextualised by a discussion of its relevance and topicality and the possible implications of the study. You may also include information about why you are interested in the topic and its relevance for your own professional development. You can try to answer the questions 'Why this?' 'Why now?' 'Why there?' 'Why me?'

Chapter 2 – Review of relevant research (20–25%)

This is an examination of relevant literature. Some key texts may be quite old, but try particularly to use recent material. Review the literature, that is, compare and contrast approaches taken. Do not argue with the ideas in your readings on the basis of anecdotal evidence or experience. Your views can come later when you can draw on your own research evidence. Use sub-headings, possibly key words from your title, to organise this section. Pull out themes in other published research and compare them. *Do not simply describe* what has been said. You need to prove in this section that you recognise the key issues and have read much of the related research.

Chapter 3 – Design of study (10%)

This can be a relatively short chapter. You need to give background information including sampling procedures: sample size and sample features and relevant contextual information (e.g. the size of the school and number of classes, the size and functions of the hospital). The information can be given in a table format. The structure of the study needs to be made clear and justified in relation to the research question. Data collection methods are mentioned but not described or justified. The reader needs to know exactly what happened and when. A table showing the time-scale of the study can be very helpful and save precious words (see Figure 7.1).

This chapter should also indicate any weaknesses in the design that you might have noticed. These might include the fact that

Week (dates)	Data Collection	Analysis
1 Oct. 4–8	Piloted questionnaire with 3 fieldworkers	Revised questionnaire
2 Oct. 11–15	Questionnaire sent to 60 fieldworkers in x, y and z districts	Computer analysis program checked
3 Nov. 1–5	Questionnaire sent for second time to 35 field workers (non-respondees)	Initial coding categories of open-ended questions agreed

Figure 7.1 A research timetable diagram

you cannot observe your case studies over an extended period or that your sampling procedure was flawed by circumstance.

Chapter 4 – Research methods (15–20%)

This is the chapter that most excites the fervent researcher and allows practitioner researchers to demonstrate a grasp of research issues. Each data collection method used needs to be described in sufficient detail to allow replication and justified in relation to the research question. Examples of methods may be given in the text or, in the case of complete instruments, as appendices. References to the research method literature should be made. Methods of analysis should be explained and details of content analysis, if used, be given, again with use of appendices. Weaknesses in the methodology, for example using an attitude scale rather than in-depth interviewing in a large qualitative study, should be acknowledged. But you should not be over-apologetic. There are limits to what a hard-pressed practitioner can do!

Chapter 5 – Presentation of results (10–15%)

Results should be presented so that their relationship with the research question are clear and the form of presentation precise. Where hypotheses or theories have been tested, this chapter should clearly state what has been confirmed or rejected. Data need to be attached to key aspects of the hypothesis or research question and be presented so that a coherent story is told. Simple figures and tables should be used and linked with short

sentences. *Do not describe* what is already evident in a table or
figure. Extracts from interviews and observations can be used to
illustrate key themes. You need to present the data at some stage
of analysis whether they are regrouped, cross-tabulated, statistically tested or arranged thematically. Presentation often
proceeds from a general overview to a focusing on specific
elements of the results. The aim of this chapter is to present a
clear picture of the findings as a precursor to the analytic
discussion that follows in Chapter 6.

Chapter 6 – Discussion of results (25–30%)
It is often helpful to see this in three sections.

(a) Analytic discussion: examine the connections and themes
    evident in the data and relate to the hypothesis or
    research questions.

(b) Relationship to existing research: discuss your findings in
    relation to the ideas discussed in Chapters 1 and 2 and
    to the research questions.
      You may also wish to make some points on research
    methodology at this point.

(c) Relevance for practice: discuss findings in relation to
    points raised about practice in Chapter 1. Consider your
    own professional development as a result of having
    undertaken the study. Propose areas for future research
    that emanate from your research.

The progressive enquiry

It is more difficult to give chapter-by-chapter guidelines for this
kind of study as so much will depend upon the story that unfolds.
Almost all the information that is provided in the traditional
empirical model has at some point to be given in a progressive
enquiry. The theoretical frameworks provided by existing
literature interact strongly with initial observations to provide
direction to the study. Details of data collection and analysis are
important features throughout. Findings are clearly presented and
any impact they might have on design is made explicit. The
distinctions between design, method, data and analysis that are
found in the empirical format are not so clearly made. The result
is that dissertations in this mode tend to tell the story of the study
within a strong analytic framework. This framework is initially

provided by the research literature but is itself modified as it is tested against the data examined at each stage of the study.

The first chapter usually places the study in context. Relevant literature and field observations are examined and the initial research question is given and justified. The chapters that follow cover specific elements of the research. They may be devoted to individual case studies, or to different aspects of the field; for example, the respective perspectives of parents, young people, teachers and youth workers. They may focus on progressive stages of the study as the research question is continuously redefined in the light of previous analysis. Each chapter should give information on the purpose and method of data collection and analysis and an analytic account of the evidence produced. Evidence may be presented in tabular or thematic formats. Illustrative examples and vignettes are often included. The study is usually completed by a final and often lengthy chapter which pulls together the key themes as they relate to the research question, raises any methodological issues and indicates areas for further research. Practitioners using this format usually include an examination of the implication for practice in this or a separate chapter. While appearing less clear in form it is no less rigorous in intent. Consequently this format and its related research design and methodologies do require the researcher to keep analytically in control of the data throughout the presentation.

An action research study

The biggest danger in writing up action research is that you focus too much on the practice that works and too little on the analytic reflection that led you to the effective practice. Examiners, although impressed by examples of good practice, are usually looking for evidence of good action research. It is a difficult distinction for the action researcher to make as the aim of good action research is good practice. Nevertheless this emphasis on evidence of the research process is consistent with the emphasis on process and the non-prescriptive goals in action research itself.

The format of a presentation of an action research study is straightforward. But its simplicity is due mainly to the fact that it is no more than a starting point. Each action research study needs to be told in the way that preserves its own integrity. There is enormous freedom in the ways that they might be presented provided that the key attributes of clarity, logical structure and evidence outlined earlier in this chapter are evident. Examples of freedom of expression include the playlet, the poem and the video programme. Nevertheless let us tediously return to the starting point and one commonly used structure.

Chapter 1 – Introduction
This should be quite personal and draw upon your reading and observations. You need to identify the focus of your study and answer the questions 'Why now?' 'Why here?' 'Why me?' in relation to that focus.

Chapter 2 – Design and methodology
A discussion of action research drawing on the action research literature, your reasons for engaging in it and a description of your reflective diary.

The next chapters can each comprise one stage in the action research process. Each can include details of the action taken, methods of monitoring used, detailed examples of the information collected, analytic reflection in the evidence, evaluation of action and review and replanning undertaken. Reference should be made to any published research or other readings that informed your thinking, action, or analysis. These chapters are then followed by two concluding chapters.

Final Chapter I – The impact on practice
This is the evaluation chapter where you pull together information on the effectiveness of the actions taken and consider implications for future practice. You may also wish to offer counter-claims to existing understandings of good practice or other research studies.

Final Chapter II – The impact on you
What have you learnt about yourself, your own practice, your professional development? It is a very personal chapter, but it may also lead you on to a discussion of action research and perhaps the management of change or professionalism.

Abstracts, bibliographies and appendices

A well-presented dissertation has to have the following features in the order shown.

- Title page – with your name and the date of presentation,
- Rubric of the validating institution (available from your tutor),
- Acknowledgements and dedication (if you wish),
- Abstract,
- Table of contents – with chapter headings and page numbers,
- The body of the dissertation – Chapters 1 to 6 or so,
- Bibliography,
- Appendices – with numbers and titles.

The abstract

This is a summary of the study which can only be written when the study has been completed. It is *not* a statement of intent. Its purpose is to provide an outline of the aims, methods, results and implications of the study for the busy reader. It is usually between 700 and 1000 words in length. It is written in the past tense and needs to provide the following degree of detail.

The abstract

- The research question or hypothesis.

- The theoretical framework used if appropriate.

- The general design.

- The sample size and features.

- The research methods used.

- Key findings.

- Implications of the findings.

The bibliography

This contains information on all the texts referred to in the study. It should not include books or articles you have read but have not mentioned in the previous chapters. Details are presented by author in alphabetical order. This can be a time-consuming exercise which is greatly assisted by your keeping a computer or card index of references made as you write up your study. There are also some quite strict conventions relating to the presentation of a bibliography. A well-presented bibliography is a feature considered by examiners as it indicates an ord‹ approach to research and a feel for the research enterprise. The well-ordered bibliography suggests that you recognise that other researchers might wish to follow up the references you use.

Conventions vary across disciplines but we shall give you a system used by most social scientists as this is widely used by practitioner researchers.

(a) Alphabetical order
Although this seems a simple instruction there are some variables to consider. The order is alphabetical order by date.

> Smith, J. (1989)
> Smith, J. (1993)

Also single authorship has precedence over joint authorship.

> Smith, J. (1989)
> Smith, J. (1993)
> Smith, J. and Jones, F. (1989)

(b) Books
You need to give author(s), date, title (underlined or italicised), place of publication and publisher.

> Smith, J. (1989) *The Way it Was*, London: Utopia Press.
> Smith, J. (ed.) (1992) *Youth in the Inner City*, Glasgow: City Press.

(c) Chapters in books
Here you give the author of the chapter referred to in the dissertation, date, the title of the chapter, the editor(s) of the book, the title of the book (underlined), place of publication and publisher.

> Smith, J. (1993) 'Wish I Weren't Here', in F. Jones (ed.), *Troubled Times*, New York: Lucky Inc.

(d) Articles
These require author(s), date, title of article, title of journal (underlined or italicised), volume and part numbers of the journal, pages of the article.

Jones, F. (1992) 'Young and unemployed: a comparative study of the young and willing to work in London and New York', *Youth Culture*, **17**(2), pp. 171–85.

(e) Conference papers

You may have the chance to read or hear conference papers. You can reference them in the following way.

Jones, F. (1993) 'Support Networks in Youth Work', Paper at the annual Youth and Community Society Conference, Bournemouth.

(f) Theses and other unpublished papers

Here you give as much information as possible.

Jones, F. (1982) 'The transition from school: a case study of school leavers in one inner city school,' unpublished PhD thesis, University of Oldham.
Smith, J. (n.d.) 'Key features in youth unemployment', Study Group Working Paper, Dept of Youth Studies, University of Winchester.
(n.d. = no date)

Appendices

Appendices follow the bibliography and usually contain the data collection instruments, examples of raw, that is unanalysed, data such as extracts from interviews, observations or diaries. They may, if you are encouraged to do so, even include the complete reflective diary. There is therefore always the danger that too much is put into appendices. The temptation to err in this way is in part due to the fact that the number of words used in an appendix do not count in the word limit applied to the dissertation.

Before anything is placed as an appendix the necessity test needs to be applied. A set of padded superfluous appendices represents an inability to be selective and makes it difficult for the reader to find what is genuinely relevant. An appendix can usefully hold a complete interview schedule, a blank observation proforma, the categorisation and coding details used in content analysis, the full tape transcript of a short recorded conversation observed so that reference can be made in the results and discussion elements of the dissertation. Indeed, anything that adds useful depth to points made in the body of the dissertation can be put in this section. An appendix is not, however, usually the place for short pieces of analysed data. These should be placed in the dissertation itself. Longer tables may best be placed as appendices if they threaten to inhibit the flow of the chapter.

Appendices need to be numbered, titled, and placed in a logical order that matches the first reference made to them in the text. Above all don't let them dominate your presentation. They provide background illuminative information. Your dissertation demonstrates your ability to analyse and synthesise information.

Referencing in the text

There are several systems in use. We have selected that most widely used by practitioner researchers. The most important points are that you are consistent, thorough and logical in your use of the system. The main purposes of referencing are to acknowledge the sources of information that have helped to shape your own thinking and to enable a reader to find the texts you have drawn upon.

There are different ways of citing or acknowledging the work of others. You may simply refer to the work in the course of your discussion:

> *Several researchers in this area (Thomas, 1991; Williams, 1991; Roberts and Hughes, 1992) have reached similar conclusions. They seem to be indicating that...*

You may wish to take a very short direct quote from another text:

> *What Williams (1991) describes as 'foolhardy', Thomas (1991) seems to read as 'brave'.*

There is no need in this case to give page numbers. If, however, your quotation is slightly longer and from a book you should give a page number. You don't give page number references for articles as they are given in full in the bibliography:

> *Williams's description of this group of school leavers as 'foolhardy and underprepared optimists' (Williams, 1991, p. 86) does not seem to be supported by...*

Longer quotations need to be separated from the text and indented. Again page number references are given for references from books but not from articles:

One of the most damning descriptions of young people today has been provided by Williams in his discussion of personal responsibility:

> *The foolhardy and underprepared optimists who leave our schools with scant regard for their own or the Nation's future do no one any service. (Williams, 1991, p. 86)*

This indictment, however, does not withstand the counterblast offered by . . .

Some examiners dislike too many long extracts in the text as they imply lack of analysis and a magpie approach to a review chapter. All examiners look for the use made of references to develop the discussion of the main points in the chapter. They are seeking evidence that you have understood and can now play with the ideas you have met.

A good guide to what is acceptable in referencing is published material itself. You will notice that authors are rarely referred to by their first names, titles of books and articles are not usually given in the text. Footnotes are out of fashion and long extracts are kept to a minimum.

Presenting research results

Quite strict conventions, or at least expectations, also apply to the way in which data are presented. Again the concern with the form of the presentation is driven by a desire for clarity. The greatest challenge when presenting data is to provide coherence. The following are useful tips to consider.

- Restate the hypothesis or research questions before presenting the data. This serves to remind the reader and to focus your analysis.
- Move consistently from a general analytic overview to specific illustrative or finely focused analysis, that is, give the wider picture before answering detailed questions. (This rule can be broken as it sometimes helps to start with illustrative case studies as a way in.)
- Group elements of your analysis together so that specific issues are clustered and are addressed in one section and not scattered randomly through the chapter or chapters.
- Present numerical data in simple tables with any necessary additional information in keys on the same page.

- Do not overkill with figures simply because your computer can produce both pie charts and histograms from the same data.
- Do not write descriptions of tables and figures, they should speak for themselves.
- Link tables and figures with sentences that highlight similarities or contrasts or indicate the element of the research question to be next addressed.
- Only present analysed data. *Examples* of raw (unanalysed) data are a good idea, but they should be presented as appendices.

Tables

You must resist any temptation to make your tables complex. Their purpose is to present your findings quickly and more effectively than in a couple of paragraphs. So avoid multi-dimensional tables. Each table needs a reference number and a title, as you will probably refer back to it in later chapters. A numbering system that relates to the chapter in which it appears is effective. Table 2 in Chapter 3 will therefore be numbered *Table 3:2*. The title of the table should be clear. For example, *Children in the primary school sample by age and sex:*

Table 3.2   Children in the primary school sample by age and sex

Sex	Age in years	5	6	7	8	9	Total
Male		3	5	8	7	5	28
Female		4	4	7	7	6	28

You may want to show statistical significance if you have applied a statistical test to your data:

Table 5.4   Means and standard deviations for groups A and B on mathematics tests

Score on maths tests	Group A Mean	Standard deviation	Mean	Group B Standard deviation	Significance
test (I)	1.63	(2.07)	0.66	(1.48)	
test (II)	38.1	(13.25)	22.05	(15.38)	**
test (III)	18.0	(13.40)	32.89	(16.01)	**

Usually ** indicates significance at the 0.01 level and * at the 0.05 level.

Figures

These include line graphs, histograms (block graphs) and pie charts. Again our advice is keep them simple. If you are using pie charts be careful when compiling them; there are mathematical procedures to be followed. If this causes problems, be content with histograms as they serve the same purpose. Figures, like tables, need to be numbered and be given titles. If you are using a 5:1, 5:2 system in tables use letters for figures, e.g. 5.A, 5.B. The titles of figures are usually placed under the diagram.

Histograms give scope for creativity. In addition to the simple representations of frequency for which they are most obviously useful, they can be used, for example, to show changes over time.

Histograms and pie charts are essentially used to present descriptive data drawn from records of frequency. Line graphs

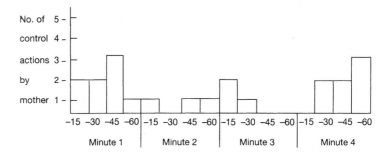

Figure 5.C Frequency of maternal control action in four minutes of interaction with a two-year-old

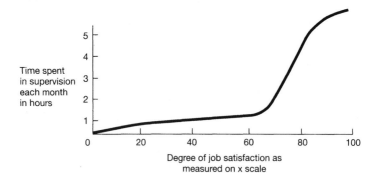

Figure 5.F The interaction between amount of supervision and degree of job satisfaction among 30 nursery nurses

can be used to present more complex data, for example to demonstrate interaction effects between continuous data sets.

Illustrative textual data

If you are presenting analysed textual data in ways which allow you to use the voices of participants, you again should be orderly in the way that you approach the task. You need to remember that you are still presenting data that have been analysed. The analysis will probably have taken the form of the identification of themes or categories as a result of content analysis. It is therefore helpful to the reader for you to start with a general listing of the themes to be illustrated. You should also give a reference to the appendices which contain your content analysis categorisation and coding instruction. You can then take each theme in turn, discuss it and illustrate the points you make with extracts from your data. The following example will give you some idea:

> *Theme One: There is no need to change*
> Sixteen of the twenty managers interviewed indicated at some point that the proposed changes were probably unnecessary. Resistance to change appears in three forms in the group: (I) we are doing what is suggested already; (II) there has been too much change – we need stability and (III) what is proposed is just a passing fashion.
>
> Seven managers reported that the change was not as novel as it appeared. The following extracts from the interviews are indicative of the feelings of this sub-group.
>
> > 'I take management seriously, think about what I do and have been working along these lines for a while now.'
> >
> > 'What is so special about what is suggested? It is what I already do.'
>
> A smaller group, only four managers, appeared to want more stability...

If you are presenting interviews or open observational data in case studies you can compile descriptive case summaries of the person or groups. The case summaries should be lively descriptions which contain the main points evident in your data. These summaries can then become your starting points for comparative case analysis and the discussion of themes. This sequence is also appropriate when you present critical incidents and vignettes. Again descriptions are followed by analytic discussion in which major patterns are teased out. It is, of course, extremely important that you protect the anonymity of your respondents when you present any form of qualitative data.

Prime concerns in the presentation of results are clarity and coherence. If done badly it can be the most difficult aspect of the dissertation for the reader to tackle; if done well it can be the most gripping.

Style

Getting the written style right can be as much a worry as actually doing the research. It should be the least of your concerns. As with any form of communication your dissertation should report honestly, openly and effectively. You demonstrate your academic ability by, for example, the way you handle the ideas of others and sort and present data, and not by writing in a stilted pseudo-academic style. Sentences therefore need to be short, informative and easy to understand.

You will need to check with your supervisor whether you should write in the first person (I tried three times to...) or in the passive (It was attempted three times). We tend to encourage the practitioners we work with to use the first person as it enables them to engage fully and personally with issues that are so often directly relevant to their own practice. However, experimental studies are usually best written in the passive. In all studies the occasional use of the passive can help alleviate the effects of the constant use of 'I'. Action research, of course *has* to be written in the first person.

Despite appearing to encourage the use of the first person we do need to emphasise that a dissertation is a place for considered thought and the use of evidence, to substantiate claims. The use of 'I think' and 'I have found' needs to be supported by evidence and not become simple assertion. 'It would seem that' and 'one likely explanation might be' or similar constructions can be used to introduce personal opinions in the tentative way often appropriate to a research enquiry.

The research report

While we have been suggesting that a dissertation is written to meet the criteria of an examination board and the national standards for academic work that it represents, we recognise that a research report required by your sponsor may be written for a variety of audiences. The first step is therefore to analyse the needs of the audiences.

A needs analysis would include:

- Who comprise the audience, for example, experts, users, politicians?
- What questions do they want answered?
- How much background information do they need?
- How simply do I need to tell the story?

The answers to these questions determine the form and the style of the presentation. Consequently a research report is usually much shorter than a dissertation. It may contain the same points, but usually in a pared-down scale. Discussion and justification of design and methodology are extensively reduced or eliminated.

Data are presented but are usually carefully selected to tell the story in an accessible way. Implications for policy and practice are considerably enhanced. A short bibliography may be included and some suggestions for additional reading may be appropriate. Appendices may be used but only if essential. For example, the questionnaire used may be appended for use by others, but it would not be usual practice to include raw data.

It is usually a good idea to write a short summary of the report of no more than two pages in which key points and implications may be presented on a bullet point format. Reference to the complete report can be made in this. These two pages will be read, presented at committee meetings, and probably have far more influence than the complete report which can be available on request.

You may wish to send your summary to a wide range of groups to stimulate interest in your findings. You could also offer workshops or training to disseminate your findings or ideas.

Getting published

The most obvious way of spreading your new-found ideas is through publication. The route to publication is not as mysterious as it might seem at the outset. The editorial teams of journals that address practitioner concerns are usually eager to receive submissions from practitioners. Consequently editors often give helpful advice and encouragement.

If you are considering publishing for the first time it is probably a good idea to consider an article as an initial endeavour. Journals have specific foci and house styles so it is useful to target your article at a particular journal. You can always change it should you be unsuccessful in your first attempt.

Attempting to get published is not a case of writing what you want to say and touting it round editors. You need a coherent plan of action which is clearly focused.

Publication action plan

(i) Identify the issues you want to make public and the angle you wish to take.

(ii) Look at the practitioner journals available.

    (a) What are the aims of each journal?

    (b) What has been published in it in the last year or so?

    (c) Do I want to write in the style used?

    (d) What guidelines are there on style and length in the notes for contributors?

    (e) Does the editorial board want an outline summary sent first, or a full paper?

(iii) Write the paper (unless a summary is requested first). Keep carefully to all the guidelines given in the 'Notes for Contributors' found in the journal.

(iv) Send the appropriate number of copies to the editor.

(v) Sit back and wait for a few months as the article is dispatched for peer review.

(vi) Either graciously accept the comments made by the reviewers and editor or discuss them further with the editor.

(vii) Amend the paper and return it to the editor.

(viii) Sit back and wait for a few months until the proofs arrive from the publisher of the journal. Make minor adjustments to the proofs if necessary and send them back.

(ix) Sit back and wait again for the final publication. From submission to publication can take a year and in some cases even longer.

By the time you read your paper in print it will seem as if it were written by someone else. Your own ideas will have developed and the context changed. Nevertheless it is important that practitioners are published and their perspectives given direct voice. So go for it!

Having an impact on practice

We have argued throughout this book that the insights that practitioner researchers gain from working with current research and investigating their own fields of practice will also inform their practices while they work in those fields. But it will be much easier to use and develop those insights while working alongside and networking with like-minded colleagues rather than struggling in isolation with colleagues who do not share the fresh perspectives. If your research is to have an impact on the practice of colleagues, that is, to change the way they interpret events and their responses to them, then it has to engage both their hearts and their minds. What better way to do that than to encourage them to examine critically current practice and the fresh insights that your research has brought, by engaging in practitioner research themselves?

We have planned several projects with practitioner researchers as two stages. In the first stage, key practitioners work together as researchers and often alongside university-based researchers to develop new understandings of practice through engaging with current research and investigating aspects of practice and networking across settings. In the second stage, these key participants are supported as they work with their immediate colleagues who, in turn, test out these understandings in their own settings and begin to incorporate new insights into their professional repertoires (see Anning and Edwards, in press 1999; Edwards in press b).

Research findings cannot simply be delivered to the sites of practice as sets of instructions to be followed. Research is a creative activity and, as such, supports practitioners as they construct and refresh the knowledge bases of their professions. In short remember, how ever hard-pressed you may feel at times, sound research is worth doing and worth talking about with colleagues.

Glossary

Attitude   Attitudes are generally regarded as a mix of both cognitive and affective aspects of understanding. They represent a reaction to phenomena. They do not, however, always direct behaviour as the social context can inhibit the motivational power of an attitude. For example racist attitudes can be tempered by a more liberal group consensus which prevents the demonstration of overt racism.

Attitude scales   These are designed to measure the strength of an attitude. Likert scales allow you to see the strength of each individual statement. Thurstone scales involve a process of careful scaling which allows you to gauge a measure of general attitude.

Baseline data   These are collected at the start of a study if the aim of the study is to discover the impact of an intervention. They are usually considered essential in any evaluation study.

Continuous data   These are data which can be seen to fall on a continuous scale, for example the score on the Thurstone Attitude Scale, a measure of temperature, an IQ score.

Control group   A control group is an essential element in an experimental study. The control group is usually closely matched in features to the experimental or treatment group. While the experimental group receives special treatment the control group received no special treatment other than the testing required to gather baseline data and final comparative data.

Datum–Data   Datum is a single item of data or information gathered in the research process. It is therefore common to talk of data as plural. Data are first seen in their raw form as, for example, questionnaire responses or an interview typescript. They are then analysed and presented in the dissertation.

Database   A database is the raw or unanalysed data which are available for further analysis.

Deduction   Deduction is the process of inference from the general to the particular. In a deductive argument the truth of the premise guarantees the truth of the conclusion. There are strong links, within research, between deductive modes of reasoning and the emphasis placed by logical positivists on the need to verify statements using systematic methods of enquiry. In research the proposition or inferred conclusion is called the hypothesis.

Evaluation   Evaluation is, at its simplest, the judgement made about the success of an action when measured against the goals that had been set for the action. Process evaluation is a variation on this which places an emphasis on what happens while the action is occurring.

Evidence-based practice   Evidence-based practice is the identification and use of research findings to inform and improve practice and to extend the knowledge-base of professional practice. Whilst based originally in medical research its use has been extended across the caring professions.

Frequency data   These are items of data which are discrete items and amenable to a simple counting. They would include the number of questions asked by a teacher, the number of times a clinic is visited, the number of references to a topic in an interview.

Grounded theory   Grounded theory is developed inductively from the content analysis of records of phenomena that occur in natural settings. The theories or frameworks produced in this way can provide new ways of seeing these phenomena.

Hegemonic practices   These are behaviours which arguably are used by the more powerful members of society to maintain their power positions within that society. Society colludes in the process by supporting the conditions that allow these behaviours and so sustains its own existing power systems.

Hypotheses and hypothesis testing   Hypotheses are propositions or statements about reality which you wish to test in your research. You may choose to use a two-tailed test or a one-tailed test. The decision depends upon your hypothesis. A two-tailed test allows you to see simply whether there is a difference between the experimental and control group. A one-tailed test allows you to test for the direction of the difference (e.g. students in group A perform better than those in group B). Consequently you can find a significant difference on a two-tailed test when no significance appears with a one-tailed test. Hypotheses are used in deductive research models. They are turned into negative predictions or null hypotheses which have to be disproved in order to verify the predictions evident in the hypotheses.

Induction   Induction is a process of inference from the particular to the general. It is used, for example, in case study research when typical cases are given as illustrative. However, most inductive forms of research apply more rigour to the process than might be implied by this simple example. The comparative analysis of cases is usually considered as essential prerequisite to sound inference. The development of grounded theory is also premised on the repeated occurrence of the particular. This is an increasingly valued approach to scientific enquiry as it allows the inductive construction of new frameworks and ways of understanding.

Logical positivism   This is an approach to research which is concerned with establishing the truth or falsity of statements. It employs the methods of observation or experiment to prove or disprove the truth of any proposition. It emphasises the importance of systematic procedures in the verification process.

Matched sample   A matched sample is a sample from a population which is matched on key variables, for example, age, social and economic status, intelligence, with another sample from the same population so that an experimental study using control and experimental groups can be undertaken.

Objectivity   In ordinary speech to be objective is to be unbiased in your treatment of established facts. In research terms, it is the belief that phenomena are guided by a system of universal laws which can be impartially observed by trained researchers. Implications of this perspective include a belief in the generalisability of research findings across different contexts, an emphasis on experimental design, and no recognition of the subjectivity of the observer/ interpreter.

Organisational development   Organisational development is the management of strategies for institutional growth and development. It is a form of management of change which keeps the development of individuals within the context of the organisation at the centre of management concerns.

Pilot study   A pilot study is usually a test-run of a data collection instrument, for example a questionnaire or interview schedule. It allows a researcher to modify any flaws in methodology prior to undertaking a major study. The study is carried out on a small (pilot) sample of people from the population under scrutiny. It should not draw on the sample to be used in the major study.

Population   A population is an identifiable group of people who share the characteristics that are to be examined. It may be all the attenders at one clinic, or all the eleven-year-olds in one school or education authority. If research findings are to be generalised to the population a sample which is considered to represent that population is selected and studied.

Proforma   A proforma is a prepared and carefully structured instrument for the manual recording of data while the researcher is in the field of study. It is usually typed on paper and aims to make the recording process as simple as possible by at least partially organising the data as they are recorded.

Qualitative methods   Qualitative research methods are those which attempt to pick up and convey the ways that the participants in the events under scrutiny make sense of them. They include some forms of observation methods, interviews and life history accounts. Data collected in this way are often presented as analytic narratives. But they can, through content analysis, be amenable to more quantitative forms of analysis. For many researchers qualitative methods serve the important function of allowing the voices of participants to be heard when the research is disseminated.

Quantitative methods   Quantitative methods of data analysis are most frequently associated with deductive research designs and the testing of hypotheses. Some forms of qualitative data collected through inductive designs are, after content analysis, also amenable to quantitative analysis. The analysis process involves the manipulation of numerical data and the application of statistical tests.

Reflective practice This is a form of continuous personal evaluation of practice carried out by practitioners on their own practice. It involves the careful examination of current practice in order to improve and develop future practice. The boundaries between reflective practice and action research are often usefully blurred. In this text we see action research to be an extended form of reflective practice in which enquiry into current practice is systematic and in which reflections are informed by interpretations that can be found in other research into that field.

Reliability Reliability is considered important in all models of research, but definitions may differ. It is essentially concerned with the consistency of the research process. In deductive models of research, reliability aims to ensure that the assessment instrument and its administration remain constant in their ability to capture the necessary information. In some inductive models of research constancy is deemed impossible and irrelevant and triangulation, or more than one perspective on a phenomenon, is seen as a source of reliability in data collection. In data analysis reliability is sought in the use of more than one analyst and measures of inter-rater reliability in the coding of data in content analysis.

Sample A sample is a group which is selected from a population and which is considered to be representative of the wider population. Findings from work from the sample can then be generalised back to the population. Sampling procedure is therefore a crucial part of the selection process. Samples used by practitioner researchers are usually selected by using stratified, random or, if all else fails, convenience sampling procedures.

Sources in literature reviews Practitioner researchers are usually expected to use a mixture of primary and secondary sources in order to indicate that they are up to date in their understanding and able to work with the findings of other researchers. Primary sources are articles, reports and theses. Books, other than books of research projects, are usually considered to be secondary sources as they tend to present information in at least a semi-digested form.

Statistical significance Significance is a measure of the extent to which a result, for example, test scores for a group of students, could be achieved by chance. If the results cannot be explained by chance it is assumed, for example, that the intervention occurring in the experimental condition had an impact on the scores. Significance levels of .05 and .01 indicate degrees of confidence in the assumption that chance was not the cause. .01 is a higher degree of confidence than .05, but both levels can be read as statistically significant.

Subjectivity In ordinary speech subjectivity is the taking of a strongly personal perspective on a phenomenon. Arguably this fits ill with a research process which aims at clarification and truth-seeking. However, in the social sciences researchers are increasingly aware of the impact of their own subjectivity on the decisions made in the research process and many choose to make this explicit, for example in feminist and anti-racist research. It can also be argued that practitioner researchers should recognise the subjectivity residing in the expert frameworks they bring to the research process and make it explicit as they undertake and write up their findings.

Symbolic function The symbolic function is a term that belongs to symbolic interactionism and the work of G.H. Mead (1934); symbolic interactionists argue that social phenomena (people, situations and objects) carry particular meanings for members of social groupings. For example, the armchair nearest the fire which is the seat of the most important person in the room, and the adjustments made to a working day to allow visits from senior doctors both serve symbolic functions which are open to interpretation.

Triangulation Researchers working within inductive models of research will often use triangulation to enable them to get a purchase on the shifting realities they are trying to capture. This is particularly true of case study research where rich data are of prime concern. Triangulation involves taking more than one, and usually three, perspectives on a phenomenon. This usually occurs in practitioner research through the use of more than one research method or more than one researcher or a mixture of these.

Validity Like reliability, validity is a major concern for all researchers. A measure of the validity of research data is the extent to which it can be agreed that the research instrument has been effective in capturing what it intends to capture. In this way it comes close to the meaning of validity common in philosophy which is the truth value in statements. Validity questions for practitioner researchers include 'Does this research method get at what I want to find out?' and 'Do the data make sense, that is, have they got face validity?'

Variables In experimental research designs you will have two types of variable: independent and dependent variables. The variable that you manipulate (e.g. the amount of tuition) is called the independent variable. The dependent variable is the variable in which you would expect to see a consequent change (e.g. performance scores). You need to separate these when starting your hypothesis. And you need to be sure that you can measure both of them.

Bibliography

Adams, G.R. and Shvaneveldt, J.D. (1991) *Understanding research methods*, New York: Longman.

Anning, A. and Edwards, A. (1999, in press) *Promoting children's learning from birth to five*, Buckingham: Open University Press.

Bannister, D. and Fransella, F. (1971) *Inquiring man*, Harmondsworth: Penguin.

Bateman, R. and Gottman, J.M. (1985) *Observing interaction*, Cambridge: Cambridge University Press.

Berger, R.M. and Patchener, M.A. (1988) *Planning for research: a guide for the helping professions*, London: Sage.

Bickman, L. and Rog, J. (eds) (1998) *Handbook of applied social research methods*, London: Sage.

Bromley, D. (1986) *The case study method in psychology and related disciplines*, New York: Wiley.

Burnard, P. and Morrison, P. (1994) (2nd edn) *Nursing research in action: developing basic skills*, London: Macmillan.

Burroughs, G.E.R. (1975) (2nd edn) *Design and analysis in educational research*, Birmingham: University of Birmingham.

Carr, W. and Kemmis, S. (1986) *Becoming critical: knowledge and action research*, London: Falmer Press.

Chaiklin, S. (1993) Understanding the social scientific practice of understanding practice, in S. Chaiklin and J. Lave (eds) *Understanding practice: perspectives on activity and context*, Cambridge: Cambridge University Press.

Chaiklin, S. and Lave, J. (eds) (1993) *Understanding practice: perspectives on activity and context*, Cambridge: Cambridge University Press.

Clifford, C. (1997) (2nd edn) *Nursing and health care research: a skills-based introduction*, London/New York: Prentice Hall.

Cohen, L. (1976) *Educational research in classrooms and schools*, London: Harper & Row.

Davidson, J. (1970) *Outdoor recreation surveys: the design and use of questionnaires for site surveys*, London: Countryside Commission.

Denzin, N. and Lincoln, Y. (eds) (1994) *Handbook of qualitative research*, London: Sage.

Doise, W., Clemence, A. and Lorenzi-Cioldi, F. (1993) *The quantitative analysis of social representations*, Hemel Hempstead: Harvester Wheatsheaf.

Edwards, A. (in press a) Investigating the complexities of teaching and mentoring, in I. Abbott and L. Evans (eds) *The future of educational research*, London: Falmer.

Edwards, A. (in press b) Research and practice: is there a dialogue? in H. Penn (ed.) *Theory, policy and practice in early childhood services*, Buckingham: Open University Press.

Edwards, A. and Collinson, J. (1996) *Mentoring and developing practice in primary schools*, Buckingham: Open University Press.

Elliott, J. (1991) *Action research for educational change*, Buckingham: Open University Press.

Ely, M. (1991) *Doing qualitative research: circles within circles*, London: Falmer Press.

Fisher, R.A. and Yates, F. (1963) *Statistical tables for biological, agricultural and medical research*, Edinburgh: Oliver & Boyd.

Fransella, F. and Bannister, D. (1977) *A manual for repertory grid technique*, London: Academic Press.

Fransella, F. and Thomas, L. (eds) (1988) *Experimenting with personal construct psychology*, London: Routledge.

Glaser, B.G. and Strauss, A.L. (1967) *The discovery of grounded theory*, Chicago: Aldine.

Griffiths, M. and Tann, S. (1992) 'Using reflective practice to link personal and public theories', *Journal of education for teaching*, **18**(1): 69–84.

Hakin, C. (1982) *Secondary analysis in social research*, London: Allen & Unwin.

Hakin, C. (1987) *Research design: strategies and choices in the design of social research*, London: Allen & Unwin.

Hamilton, D. (1994) Traditions, preferences and postures in applied qualitative research, in N. Denzin and Y. Guba (eds) *Handbook of qualitative research*, London: Sage.

Hammersley, M. (1992) *What's wrong with ethnography?*, London: Routledge.

Heyes, S., Hardy, M., Humphreys, P. and Rookes, P. (1986) *Starting statistics in psychology and education: a student handbook*, London: Weidenfeld & Nicolson.

Hopkins, D. (1993) (2nd edn) *A teachers' guide to classroom research*, Buckingham: Open University Press.

Huberman, M. (1995) 'Networks that alter teaching', *Teachers and teaching: theory and practice*, **1**(2): 193–211.

Kelly, G.A. (1955) *The psychology of personal constructs*, New York: Norton.

Kiess, H.O. and Bloomquist, D.W. (1985) *Psychological research methods: a conceptual approach*, Boston: Allyn & Bacon.

King, E. (1987) *How to use a library: a guide for young people and students*, Plymouth: Northcote House.

Kinnear, P. and Gray, C. (1994) *SPSS for Windows made simple*, London: Lawrence Erlbaum Asssociates.

Krippendorff, K. (1980) *Content analysis: an introduction to its methodology*, London: Sage.

McGee, P. and Notter, J. (1995) *Research appreciation: an initial guide for nurses and health care professionals*, Dinton: Quay Books

McNiff, J. (1993) *Teaching as learning*, London: Routledge.

Mead, G.H. (1934) *Mind, self and society*, Chicago: University of Chicago Press.

Miller, J. (1990) *Creating spaces and finding voices*, New York: SUNY.

Moore, N. (1987) (2nd edn) *How to do research*, London: Library Association.

Moser, C.A. and Kalton, G. (1977) *Survey methods in social investigation*, Oxford: Heinemann.

Oppenheim, A.N. (1992) *Questionnaire design, interviewing and attitude measurement*, London: Pinter.

Pellegrini, A. (1991) *Applied child study: a developmental approach*, London: Lawrence Erlbaum Associates.

Platt, J. (1981) 'Evidence and proof in documentary research', *Sociological review*, **29**: 31–66.

Reed, J. and Procter, S. (eds) (1995) *Practitioner research in health care*, London: Chapman & Hall

Robson C. (1994) *Experiment, design and statistics in psychology*, Harmondsworth: Penguin.

Siegel, S. (1956) *Nonparametric statistics for the behavioural sciences*, New York: McGraw-Hill.

Stake, R. (1994) Case studies, in N. Denzin and Y. Guba (eds) *Handbook of qualitative research*, London: Sage.

Stenhouse, L. (1975) *An introduction to curriculum research and development*, Oxford: Heinemann.

Stevens, S.S. (1946) 'On the theory of scales of measurement', *Science*, **103**: 677–80.

Stevens, S.S. (1951) 'Mathematics, measurement and psychophysics', in S.S. Stevens (ed.) *Handbook of experimental psychology*, New York: Wiley.

Stewart, D. and Shamdasani, P. (1990) *Focus Groups: theory and practice*, London: Sage.

Stewart, D. and Shamdasani, P. (1998) Focus groups: exploration and discovery, in L. Bickman and D. Rog (eds) *Handbook of applied social research methods*, London: Sage.

Sylva, K.D., Roy, C. and Painter, M. (1980) *Childwatching at playgroup and nursery school*, Oxford: Grant McIntyre.

Taylor, C. (1977) 'What is human agency?', in T. Mischel (ed.)· *The self: psychological and philosophical issues*, Oxford: Blackwell.

Upshaw, H.S. (1968) 'Attitude measurement', in H.M. Blalock and A.B. Blalock (eds) *Methodology in social research*, New York: McGraw-Hill.

Whittaker, K. (1972) *Using libraries: an informative guide for students and general users*, London: André Deutsch.

Wilkinson, R.G. (1986) *Class and health: research and longitudinal data*, London: Tavistock.

Winship, I. and McNab, A. (1996) *The students' guide to the Internet*, London: Library Association Publishing.

Yin, R. (1998) The abridged version of case study research: design and method, in L. Bickman and D. Rog (eds) *Handbook of applied social research methods*, London: Sage.

Appendices

Appendix A
Z values and proportions of values under the normal curve

z value	Area between mean and z value	Area beyond z value	z value	Area between mean and z value	Area beyond z value
0.00	0.0000	0.5000	0.45	0.1736	0.3264
0.01	0.0040	0.4960	0.46	0.1772	0.3228
0.02	0.0080	0.4920	0.47	0.1808	0.3192
0.03	0.0120	0.4880	0.48	0.1844	0.3156
0.04	0.0160	0.4840	0.49	0.1879	0.3121
0.05	0.0199	0.4801	0.50	0.1915	0.3085
0.06	0.0239	0.4761	0.51	0.1950	0.3050
0.07	0.0279	0.4721	0.52	0.1983	0.3015
0.08	0.0319	0.4681	0.53	0.2019	0.2981
0.09	0.0359	0.4641	0.54	0.2054	0.2946
0.10	0.0398	0.4602	0.55	0.2088	0.2912
0.11	0.0438	0.4562	0.56	0.2123	0.2877
0.12	0.0478	0.4522	0.57	0.2157	0.2843
0.13	0.0517	0.4483	0.58	0.2190	0.2810
0.14	0.0557	0.4443	0.59	0.2224	0.2776
0.15	0.0596	0.4404	0.60	0.2257	0.2743
0.16	0.0636	0.4364	0.61	0.2291	0.2709
0.17	0.0675	0.4325	0.62	0.2324	0.2676
0.18	0.0714	0.4286	0.63	0.2357	0.2643
0.19	0.0753	0.4247	0.64	0.2389	0.2611
0.20	0.0793	0.4207	0.65	0.2422	0.2578
0.21	0.0832	0.4168	0.66	0.2454	0.2546
0.22	0.0871	0.4129	0.67	0.2486	0.2514
0.23	0.0910	0.4090	0.68	0.2517	0.2483
0.24	0.0948	0.4052	0.69	0.2549	0.2451
0.25	0.0987	0.4013	0.70	0.2580	0.2420
0.26	0.1026	0.3974	0.71	0.2611	0.2389
0.27	0.1064	0.3936	0.72	0.2642	0.2358
0.28	0.1103	0.3897	0.73	0.2673	0.2327
0.29	0.1141	0.3859	0.74	0.2704	0.2296
0.30	0.1179	0.3821	0.75	0.2734	0.2266
0.31	0.1217	0.3783	0.76	0.2764	0.2236
0.32	0.1255	0.3745	0.77	0.2794	0.2206
0.33	0.1293	0.3707	0.78	0.2823	0.2177
0.34	0.1331	0.3669	0.79	0.2852	0.2148
0.35	0.1368	0.3632	0.80	0.2881	0.2119
0.36	0.1406	0.3594	0.81	0.2910	0.2090
0.37	0.1443	0.3557	0.82	0.2939	0.2061
0.38	0.1480	0.3520	0.83	0.2967	0.2033
0.39	0.1517	0.3483	0.84	0.2995	0.2005
0.40	0.1554	0.3446	0.85	0.3023	0.1977
0.41	0.1591	0.3409	0.86	0.3051	0.1949
0.42	0.1628	0.3372	0.87	0.3078	0.1922
0.43	0.1664	0.3336	0.88	0.3106	0.1894
0.44	0.1700	0.3300	0.89	0.3133	0.1867

Appendix A (*cont.*)
Z values and proportions of values under the normal curve

z value	Area between mean and z value	Area beyond z value	z value	Area between mean and z value	Area beyond z value
0.90	0.3159	0.1841	1.35	0.4115	0.0885
0.91	0.3186	0.1814	1.36	0.4131	0.0869
0.92	0.3212	0.1788	1.37	0.4147	0.0853
0.93	0.3238	0.1762	1.38	0.4162	0.0838
0.94	0.3264	0.1736	1.39	0.4177	0.0823
0.95	0.3289	0.1711	1.40	0.4192	0.0808
0.96	0.3315	0.1685	1.41	0.4207	0.0793
0.97	0.3340	0.1660	1.42	0.4222	0.0778
0.98	0.3365	0.1635	1.43	0.4236	0.0764
0.99	0.3389	0.1611	1.44	0.4251	0.0749
1.00	0.3413	0.1587	1.45	0.4265	0.0735
1.01	0.3438	0.1562	1.46	0.4279	0.0721
1.02	0.3461	0.1539	1.47	0.4292	0.0708
1.03	0.3485	0.1515	1.48	0.4306	0.0694
1.04	0.3508	0.1492	1.49	0.4319	0.0681
1.05	0.3531	0.1469	1.50	0.4332	0.0668
1.06	0.3554	0.1446	1.51	0.4345	0.0655
1.07	0.3577	0.1423	1.52	0.4357	0.0643
1.08	0.3599	0.1401	1.53	0.4370	0.0630
1.09	0.3621	0.1379	1.54	0.4382	0.0618
1.10	0.3643	0.1357	1.55	0.4394	0.0606
1.11	0.3665	0.1335	1.56	0.4406	0.0594
1.12	0.3686	0.1314	1.57	0.4418	0.0582
1.13	0.3708	0.1292	1.58	0.4429	0.0571
1.14	0.3729	0.1271	1.59	0.4441	0.0559
1.15	0.3749	0.1251	1.60	0.4452	0.0548
1.16	0.3770	0.1230	1.61	0.4463	0.0537
1.17	0.3790	0.1210	1.62	0.4474	0.0526
1.18	0.3810	0.1190	1.63	0.4484	0.0516
1.19	0.3830	0.1170	1.64	0.4495	0.0505
1.20	0.3849	0.1151	1.65	0.4505	0.0495
1.21	0.3869	0.1131	1.66	0.4515	0.0485
1.22	0.3888	0.1112	1.67	0.4525	0.0475
1.23	0.3907	0.1093	1.68	0.4535	0.0465
1.24	0.3925	0.1075	1.69	0.4545	0.0455
1.25	0.3944	0.1056	1.70	0.4554	0.0446
1.26	0.3962	0.1038	1.71	0.4564	0.0436
1.27	0.3980	0.1020	1.72	0.4573	0.0427
1.28	0.3997	0.1003	1.73	0.4582	0.0418
1.29	0.4015	0.0985	1.74	0.4591	0.0409
1.30	0.4032	0.0968	1.75	0.4599	0.0401
1.31	0.4049	0.0951	1.76	0.4608	0.0392
1.32	0.4066	0.0934	1.77	0.4616	0.0384
1.33	0.4082	0.0918	1.78	0.4625	0.0375
1.34	0.4099	0.0901	1.79	0.4633	0.0367

Appendix A (*cont.*)

Z values and proportions of values under the normal curve

z value	Area between mean and z value	Area beyond z value	z value	Area between mean and z value	Area beyond z value
1.80	0.4641	0.0359	2.25	0.4878	0.0122
1.81	0.4649	0.0351	2.26	0.4881	0.0119
1.82	0.4656	0.0344	2.27	0.4884	0.0116
1.83	0.4664	0.0336	2.28	0.4887	0.0113
1.84	0.4671	0.0329	2.29	0.4890	0.0110
1.85	0.4678	0.0322	2.30	0.4893	0.0107
1.86	0.4686	0.0314	2.31	0.4896	0.0104
1.87	0.4693	0.0307	2.32	0.4898	0.0102
1.88	0.4699	0.0301	2.33	0.4901	0.0099
1.89	0.4706	0.0294	2.34	0.4904	0.0096
1.90	0.4713	0.0287	2.35	0.4906	0.0094
1.91	0.4719	0.0281	2.36	0.4909	0.0091
1.92	0.4726	0.0274	2.37	0.4911	0.0089
1.93	0.4732	0.0268	2.38	0.4913	0.0087
1.94	0.4738	0.0262	2.39	0.4916	0.0084
1.95	0.4744	0.0256	2.40	0.4918	0.0082
1.96	0.4750	0.0250	2.41	0.4920	0.0080
1.97	0.4756	0.0244	2.42	0.4922	0.0078
1.98	0.4761	0.0239	2.43	0.4925	0.0075
1.99	0.4767	0.0233	2.44	0.4927	0.0073
2.00	0.4772	0.0228	2.45	0.4929	0.0071
2.01	0.4778	0.0222	2.46	0.4931	0.0069
2.02	0.4783	0.0217	2.47	0.4932	0.0068
2.03	0.4788	0.0212	2.48	0.4934	0.0066
2.04	0.4793	0.0207	2.49	0.4936	0.0064
2.05	0.4798	0.0202	2.50	0.4938	0.0062
2.06	0.4803	0.0197	2.51	0.4940	0.0060
2.07	0.4808	0.0192	2.52	0.4941	0.0059
2.08	0.4812	0.0188	2.53	0.4943	0.0057
2.09	0.4817	0.0183	2.54	0.4945	0.0055
2.10	0.4821	0.0179	2.55	0.4946	0.0054
2.11	0.4826	0.0174	2.56	0.4948	0.0052
2.12	0.4830	0.0170	2.57	0.4949	0.0051
2.13	0.4834	0.0166	2.58	0.4951	0.0049
2.14	0.4838	0.0162	2.59	0.4952	0.0048
2.15	0.4842	0.0158	2.60	0.4953	0.0047
2.16	0.4846	0.0154	2.61	0.4955	0.0045
2.17	0.4850	0.0150	2.62	0.4956	0.0044
2.18	0.4854	0.0146	2.63	0.4957	0.0043
2.19	0.4857	0.0143	2.64	0.4959	0.0041
2.20	0.4861	0.0139	2.65	0.4960	0.0040
2.21	0.4864	0.0136	2.66	0.4961	0.0039
2.22	0.4868	0.0132	2.67	0.4962	0.0038
2.23	0.4871	0.0129	2.68	0.4963	0.0037
2.24	0.4875	0.0125	2.69	0.4964	0.0036

Appendix A (*cont.*)
Z values and proportions of values under the normal curve

z value	Area between mean and z value	Area beyond z value	z value	Area between mean and z value	Area beyond z value
2.70	0.4965	0.0035	3.05	0.4989	0.0011
2.71	0.4966	0.0034	3.06	0.4989	0.0011
2.72	0.4967	0.0033	3.07	0.4989	0.0011
2.73	0.4968	0.0032	3.08	0.4990	0.0010
2.74	0.4969	0.0031	3.09	0.4990	0.0010
2.75	0.4970	0.0030	3.10	0.4990	0.0010
2.76	0.4971	0.0029	3.11	0.4991	0.0009
2.77	0.4972	0.0028	3.12	0.4991	0.0009
2.78	0.4973	0.0027	3.13	0.4991	0.0009
2.79	0.4974	0.0026	3.14	0.4992	0.0008
2.80	0.4974	0.0026	3.15	0.4992	0.0008
2.81	0.4975	0.0025	3.16	0.4992	0.0008
2.82	0.4976	0.0024	3.17	0.4992	0.0008
2.83	0.4977	0.0023	3.18	0.4993	0.0007
2.84	0.4977	0.0023	3.19	0.4993	0.0007
2.85	0.4978	0.0022	3.20	0.4993	0.0007
2.86	0.4979	0.0021	3.21	0.4993	0.0007
2.87	0.4979	0.0021	3.22	0.4994	0.0006
2.88	0.4980	0.0020	3.23	0.4994	0.0006
2.89	0.4981	0.0019	3.24	0.4994	0.0006
2.90	0.4981	0.0019	3.25	0.4994	0.0006
2.91	0.4982	0.0018	3.30	0.4995	0.0005
2.92	0.4982	0.0018	3.35	0.4996	0.0004
2.93	0.4983	0.0017	3.40	0.4997	0.0003
2.94	0.4984	0.0016	3.45	0.4997	0.0003
2.95	0.4984	0.0016	3.50	0.4998	0.0002
2.96	0.4985	0.0015	3.60	0.4998	0.0002
2.97	0.4985	0.0015	3.70	0.4999	0.0001
2.98	0.4986	0.0014	3.80	0.4999	0.0001
2.99	0.4986	0.0014	3.90	0.49995	0.00005
3.00	0.4987	0.0013	4.00	0.49997	0.00003
3.01	0.4987	0.0013			
3.02	0.4987	0.0013			
3.03	0.4988	0.0012			
3.04	0.4988	0.0012			

(Adapted from Table IIi, Fisher, R.A. and Yates, F. 1963. *Statistical tables for biological, agricultural and medical research*, 6th edn, Oliver & Boyd)

Appendix B

Values of Pearson's r Correlation Coefficient for different levels of significance

N–2	0.05	0.01	0.001
1	0.99692	0.999877	0.9999988
2	0.95000	0.990000	0.99900
3	0.8783	0.95873	0.99116
4	0.8114	0.91720	0.97406
5	0.7545	0.8745	0.95074
6	0.7067	0.8343	0.92493
7	0.6664	0.7977	0.8982
8	0.6319	0.7646	0.8721
9	0.6021	0.7348	0.8471
10	0.5760	0.7079	0.8233
11	0.5529	0.6835	0.8010
12	0.5324	0.6614	0.7800
13	0.5139	0.6411	0.7603
14	0.4973	0.6226	0.7420
15	0.4821	0.6055	0.7246
16	0.4683	0.5897	0.7084
17	0.4555	0.5751	0.6932
18	0.4438	0.5614	0.6787
19	0.4329	0.5487	0.6652
20	0.4227	0.5368	0.6524
25	0.3809	0.4860	0.6074
30	0.3494	0.4487	0.5541
35	0.3246	0.4182	0.5189
40	0.3044	0.3932	0.4806
45	0.2875	0.3721	0.4648
50	0.2732	0.3541	0.4433
60	0.2500	0.3248	0.4073
70	0.2310	0.3017	0.3799
80	0.2172	0.2830	0.3568
90	0.2050	0.2673	0.3375
100	0.1946	0.2540	0.3211

(Adapted from Table VII, Fisher, R.A. and Yates, F. 1963. *Statistical tables for biological, agricultural and medical research*, 6th edn, Oliver & Boyd)

Appendix C
Critical values of Spearman's Rank-Order Correlation Coefficient

	Significance level	
N	0.05	0.01
4	1.000	
5	0.900	1.000
6	0.829	0.943
7	0.714	0.893
8	0.643	0.833
9	0.600	0.783
10	0.564	0.746
12	0.506	0.712
14	0.456	0.645
16	0.425	0.601
18	0.399	0.564
20	0.377	0.534
22	0.359	0.508
24	0.343	0.485
26	0.329	0.465
28	0.317	0.448
30	0.306	0.432

For numbers of pairs greater than $N = 30$ the critical value of the correlation coefficient alters only slightly.
(Adapted from Table P, Siegel, S. 1956. *Nonparametric statistics for the behavioural sciences*, McGraw-Hill)

Appendix D   Table of critical values χ^2

Degrees of freedom	Levels of significance		
	0.05	0.01	0.001
1	3.84	6.64	10.83
2	5.99	9.21	13.82
3	7.82	11.34	16.27
4	9.49	13.28	18.46
5	11.07	15.09	20.52
6	12.59	16.81	22.46
7	14.07	18.48	24.32
8	15.51	20.09	26.12
9	16.92	21.67	27.88
10	18.31	23.21	29.59
11	19.68	24.72	31.26
12	21.03	26.22	32.91
13	22.36	27.69	34.53
14	23.68	29.14	36.12
15	25.00	30.58	37.70
16	26.3	32.0	39.25
17	27.6	33.4	40.79
18	28.9	34.8	42.31
19	30.1	36.2	43.82
20	31.4	37.6	45.32

(Adapted from Table IV, Fisher, R.A. and Yates, F. 1963. *Statistical tables for biological, agricultural and medical research*, 6th edn, Oliver & Boyd)

Appendix E

Critical values of Mann–Whitney U test (significance level of 0.05, two-tailed test)

n_2 \ n_1	2	3	4	5	6	7	8	9	10
2	–	–	–	–	–	–	0/16	0/18	0/20
3	–	–	–	0/15	1/17	1/20	2/22	2/25	3/27
4	–	–	0/16	1/19	2/22	3/25	4/28	4/32	5/35
5	–	0/15	1/19	2/23	3/27	5/30	6/34	7/38	8/42
6	–	1/17	2/22	3/27	5/31	6/36	8/40	10/44	11/49
7	–	1/20	3/25	5/30	6/36	8/41	10/46	12/51	14/56
8	0/16	2/22	4/28	6/34	8/40	10/46	13/51	15/57	17/63
9	0/18	2/25	4/32	7/38	10/44	12/51	15/57	17/64	20/70
10	0/20	3/27	5/35	8/42	11/49	14/56	17/63	20/70	23/77
11	0/22	3/30	6/38	9/46	13/53	16/61	19/69	23/76	26/84
12	1/23	4/32	7/41	11/49	14/58	18/66	22/74	26/82	29/91
13	1/25	4/35	8/44	12/53	16/62	20/71	24/80	28/89	33/97
14	1/27	5/37	9/47	13/53	17/62	22/71	26/80	31/89	36/97
15	1/27	5/37	10/47	14/51	19/67	24/76	29/86	34/95	39/104
16	1/29	6/40	11/50	15/61	21/71	26/81	31/91	37/101	42/111
17	2/31	6/42	11/53	17/65	22/75	28/86	34/97	39/107	45/118
18	2/32	7/45	12/57	18/68	24/80	30/91	36/102	42/114	48/125
19	2/34	7/47	13/60	19/72	25/84	32/96	38/108	45/120	52/132
20	2/36	8/50	13/63	20/76	27/89	34/101	41/114	48/126	55/138
	38	52	67	80	93	106	119	132	145

(Dashes in the table indicate that no decision is possible at the stated level of significance.) When either n_1 or n_2 is one, the test is not possible.

Appendix E (*cont.*)
Critical values of Mann–Whitney U test (significance level of 0.05, two-tailed test)

11	12	13	14	15	16	17	18	19	20
0	1	1	1	1	1	2	2	2	2
22	23	25	27	29	31	32	34	36	37
3	4	4	5	5	6	6	7	7	8
30	32	35	37	40	42	45	47	50	52
6	7	8	9	10	11	11	12	13	13
38	41	44	47	50	53	57	60	63	67
9	11	12	13	14	15	17	18	19	20
46	49	53	57	61	65	68	72	76	80
13	14	16	17	19	21	22	24	25	27
53	58	62	67	71	75	80	84	89	93
16	18	20	22	24	26	28	30	32	34
61	66	71	76	81	86	91	96	101	106
19	22	24	26	29	31	34	36	38	41
69	74	80	86	91	97	102	108	111	119
23	26	28	31	34	37	39	42	45	48
76	82	89	95	101	107	114	120	126	132
26	29	33	36	39	42	45	48	52	55
84	91	97	104	111	118	125	132	138	145
30	33	37	40	44	47	51	55	58	62
91	99	106	114	121	129	136	143	151	158
33	37	41	45	49	53	57	61	65	69
99	107	115	123	131	139	147	155	163	171
37	41	45	50	54	59	63	67	72	76
106	115	124	132	141	149	158	167	175	184
40	45	50	55	59	64	67	74	78	83
114	123	132	141	151	160	171	178	188	197
44	49	54	59	64	70	75	80	85	90
121	131	141	151	161	170	180	190	200	210
47	53	59	64	70	75	81	86	92	98
129	139	149	160	170	181	191	202	212	222
51	57	63	67	75	81	87	93	99	105
136	147	158	171	180	191	202	213	224	235
55	61	67	74	80	86	93	99	106	112
143	155	167	178	190	202	213	225	236	248
58	65	72	78	85	92	99	106	113	119
151	163	175	188	200	212	224	236	248	261
62	69	76	83	90	98	105	112	119	127
158	171	184	197	210	222	235	248	261	273

Appendix E (*cont.*)

Mann–Whitney U test (significance level of 0.05, one-tailed test)

n_2 \ n_1	1	2	3	4	5	6	7	8	9
1	–	–	–	–	–	–	–	–	–
2	–	–	–	–	0	0	0	1	1
					10	12	14	15	17
3	–	–	0	0	1	2	2	3	3
			9	12	14	16	19	21	24
4	–	–	0	1	2	3	4	5	6
			12	15	18	21	24	27	30
5	–	0	1	2	4	5	6	8	9
		10	14	18	21	25	29	32	36
6	–	0	2	3	5	7	8	10	12
		12	16	21	25	29	34	38	42
7	–	0	2	4	6	8	11	13	15
		14	19	24	29	34	38	43	48
8	–	1	3	5	8	10	13	15	18
		15	21	27	32	38	43	49	54
9	–	1	3	6	9	12	15	18	21
		17	24	30	36	42	48	54	60
10	–	1	4	7	11	14	17	20	24
		19	26	33	39	46	53	60	66
11	–	1	5	8	12	16	19	23	27
		21	28	36	43	50	58	65	72
12	–	2	5	9	13	17	21	26	30
		22	31	39	47	55	63	70	78
13	–	2	6	10	15	19	24	28	33
		24	33	42	50	59	67	76	84
14	–	2	7	11	16	21	26	31	36
		26	35	45	54	63	72	81	90
15	–	3	7	12	18	23	28	33	39
		27	38	48	57	67	77	87	96
16	–	3	8	14	19	25	30	36	42
		29	40	50	61	71	82	92	102
17	–	3	9	15	20	26	33	39	45
		31	42	53	65	76	86	97	108
18	–	4	9	16	22	28	35	41	48
		32	45	56	68	80	91	103	114
19	0	4	10	17	23	30	37	44	51
	19	34	47	59	72	84	96	108	120
20	0	4	11	18	25	32	39	47	54
	20	36	49	62	75	88	101	113	126

(Dashes in the table indicate that no decision is possible at the stated level of significance.)

(Adapted from Tables J and K, Siegel, S. 1956. *Nonparametric statistics for the behavioural sciences*, McGraw-Hill)

Appendix E (*cont.*)
Mann–Whitney U test (significance level of 0.05, one-tailed test)

10	11	12	13	14	15	16	17	18	19	20
–	–	–	–	–	–	–	–	–	0/19	0/20
1/19	1/21	2/22	2/24	2/26	3/27	3/29	3/31	4/32	4/34	4/36
4/26	5/28	5/31	6/33	7/35	7/38	8/40	9/42	9/45	10/47	11/49
7/33	8/36	9/39	10/42	11/45	12/48	14/50	15/53	16/56	17/59	18/62
11/39	12/43	13/47	15/50	16/54	18/57	19/61	20/65	22/68	23/72	25/75
14/46	16/50	17/55	19/59	21/63	23/67	25/71	26/76	28/80	30/84	32/88
17/53	19/58	21/63	24/67	26/72	28/77	30/82	33/86	35/91	37/96	39/101
20/60	23/65	26/70	28/76	31/81	33/87	36/92	39/97	41/103	44/108	47/113
24/66	27/72	30/78	33/84	36/90	39/96	42/102	45/108	48/114	51/120	54/126
27/73	31/79	34/86	37/93	41/99	44/106	48/112	51/119	55/125	58/132	62/138
31/79	34/87	38/94	42/101	46/108	50/115	54/122	57/130	61/137	65/144	69/151
34/86	38/94	42/102	47/109	51/117	55/125	60/132	64/140	68/148	72/156	77/163
37/93	42/101	47/109	51/118	56/126	61/134	65/143	70/151	75/159	80/167	84/176
41/99	46/108	51/117	56/126	61/135	66/144	71/153	77/161	82/170	87/179	92/188
44/106	50/115	55/125	61/134	66/144	72/153	77/163	83/172	88/182	94/191	100/200
48/112	54/122	60/132	65/143	71/153	77/163	83/173	89/183	95/193	101/203	107/213
51/119	57/130	64/140	70/151	77/161	83/172	89/183	96/193	102/204	109/214	115/225
55/123	61/137	68/148	75/159	82/170	88/182	95/193	102/204	109/215	116/226	123/237
58/132	65/144	72/156	80/167	87/179	94/191	101/203	109/214	116/226	123/238	130/250
62/138	69/151	77/163	84/176	92/188	100/200	107/213	115/225	123/237	130/250	138/262

Appendix E (*cont.*)

Mann–Whitney U test (significance level of 0.01, two-tailed test)

Each cell gives the two critical values (lower / upper).

n_2 \ n_1	2	3	4	5	6	7	8	9	10
2	–	–	–	–	–	–	–	–	–
3	–	–	–	–	–	–	–	0/27	0/30
4	–	–	–	–	0/24	0/28	1/31	1/35	2/38
5	–	–	–	0/25	1/29	1/34	2/38	3/42	4/46
6	–	–	0/24	1/29	2/34	3/39	4/44	5/49	6/54
7	–	–	0/28	1/34	3/39	4/45	6/50	7/56	9/61
8	–	–	1/31	2/38	4/44	6/50	7/57	9/63	11/69
9	–	0/27	1/35	3/42	5/49	7/56	9/63	11/70	13/77
10	–	0/30	2/38	4/46	6/54	9/61	11/69	13/77	16/84
11	–	0/33	2/42	5/50	7/59	10/67	13/75	16/83	18/92
12	–	1/35	3/45	6/54	9/63	12/72	15/81	18/90	21/99
13	–	1/38	3/49	7/58	10/68	13/78	17/87	20/97	24/106
14	–	1/41	4/52	7/63	11/73	15/83	18/94	22/104	26/114
15	–	2/43	5/55	8/67	12/78	16/89	20/100	24/111	29/121
16	–	2/46	5/59	9/71	13/83	18/94	22/106	27/117	31/129
17	–	2/49	6/62	10/75	15/87	19/100	24/112	29/124	34/136
18	–	2/52	6/66	11/79	16/92	21/105	26/118	31/131	37/143
19	0/38	3/54	7/69	12/83	17/97	22/111	28/124	33/138	39/151
20	0/40	3/57	8/72	13/87	18/102	24/116	30/130	36/144	42/158

(Dashes in the table indicate that no decision is possible at the stated level of significance.) When either n_1 or n_2 is one, the test is not possible.

Appendix E (*cont.*)

Mann–Whitney U test (significance level of 0.01, two-tailed test)

11	12	13	14	15	16	17	18	19	20
—	—	—	—	—	—	—	—	0/38	0/40
0/33	1/35	1/38	1/41	2/43	2/46	2/49	2/52	3/54	3/57
2/42	3/45	3/49	4/42	5/55	5/59	6/62	6/66	7/69	8/72
5/50	6/54	7/58	7/63	8/67	9/71	10/75	11/79	12/83	13/87
7/59	9/63	10/68	11/73	12/78	13/83	15/87	16/92	17/97	18/102
10/67	12/72	13/78	15/83	16/89	18/94	19/100	21/105	22/111	24/116
13/75	15/81	17/87	18/94	20/100	22/106	24/112	26/118	28/124	30/130
16/83	18/90	20/97	22/104	24/111	27/117	29/124	31/131	33/138	36/144
18/92	21/99	24/106	26/114	29/121	31/129	34/136	37/143	39/151	42/158
21/100	24/108	27/116	30/124	33/132	36/140	39/148	42/156	45/164	48/172
24/108	27/117	31/125	34/134	37/143	41/151	44/160	47/169	51/177	54/186
27/116	31/125	34/125	38/144	42/153	45/163	49/172	53/181	56/191	60/200
30/124	34/134	38/144	42/154	46/164	50/174	54/184	58/194	63/203	67/213
33/132	37/143	42/153	46/164	51/174	55/185	60/195	64/206	69/216	73/227
36/140	41/151	45/163	50/174	55/185	60/196	65/207	70/218	74/230	79/241
39/148	44/160	49/172	54/184	60/195	65/207	70/219	75/231	81/242	86/254
42/156	47/169	53/181	58/194	64/206	70/218	75/231	81/243	87/255	92/268
45/164	51/177	56/191	63/203	69/216	74/230	81/242	87/255	93/168	99/281
48/172	54/186	60/200	67/213	73/227	79/241	86/254	92/268	99/281	105/295

Appendix E (*cont.*)

Mann–Whitney U test (significance level of 0.01, one-tailed test)

n_2 \ n_1	2	3	4	5	6	7	8	9	10
2	–	–	–	–	–	–	–	–	–
3	–	–	–	–	–	$\frac{0}{21}$	$\frac{0}{24}$	$\frac{1}{26}$	$\frac{1}{29}$
4	–	–	–	$\frac{0}{20}$	$\frac{1}{23}$	$\frac{1}{27}$	$\frac{2}{30}$	$\frac{3}{33}$	$\frac{3}{37}$
5	–	–	$\frac{0}{20}$	$\frac{1}{24}$	$\frac{2}{28}$	$\frac{3}{32}$	$\frac{4}{36}$	$\frac{5}{40}$	$\frac{6}{44}$
6	–	–	$\frac{1}{23}$	$\frac{2}{28}$	$\frac{3}{33}$	$\frac{4}{38}$	$\frac{6}{42}$	$\frac{7}{47}$	$\frac{8}{52}$
7	–	$\frac{0}{21}$	$\frac{1}{27}$	$\frac{3}{32}$	$\frac{4}{38}$	$\frac{6}{43}$	$\frac{7}{49}$	$\frac{9}{54}$	$\frac{11}{59}$
8	–	$\frac{0}{24}$	$\frac{2}{30}$	$\frac{4}{36}$	$\frac{6}{42}$	$\frac{7}{49}$	$\frac{9}{55}$	$\frac{11}{61}$	$\frac{13}{67}$
9	–	$\frac{1}{26}$	$\frac{3}{33}$	$\frac{5}{40}$	$\frac{7}{47}$	$\frac{9}{54}$	$\frac{11}{61}$	$\frac{14}{67}$	$\frac{16}{74}$
10	–	$\frac{1}{29}$	$\frac{3}{37}$	$\frac{6}{44}$	$\frac{8}{52}$	$\frac{11}{59}$	$\frac{13}{67}$	$\frac{16}{74}$	$\frac{19}{81}$
11	–	$\frac{1}{32}$	$\frac{4}{40}$	$\frac{7}{48}$	$\frac{9}{57}$	$\frac{12}{65}$	$\frac{15}{73}$	$\frac{18}{81}$	$\frac{22}{88}$
12	–	$\frac{2}{34}$	$\frac{5}{43}$	$\frac{8}{52}$	$\frac{11}{61}$	$\frac{14}{70}$	$\frac{17}{79}$	$\frac{21}{87}$	$\frac{24}{96}$
13	$\frac{0}{26}$	$\frac{2}{37}$	$\frac{5}{47}$	$\frac{9}{56}$	$\frac{12}{66}$	$\frac{16}{75}$	$\frac{20}{84}$	$\frac{23}{94}$	$\frac{27}{103}$
14	$\frac{0}{28}$	$\frac{2}{40}$	$\frac{6}{50}$	$\frac{10}{60}$	$\frac{13}{71}$	$\frac{17}{81}$	$\frac{22}{90}$	$\frac{26}{100}$	$\frac{30}{110}$
15	$\frac{0}{30}$	$\frac{3}{42}$	$\frac{7}{53}$	$\frac{11}{64}$	$\frac{15}{75}$	$\frac{19}{86}$	$\frac{24}{96}$	$\frac{28}{107}$	$\frac{33}{117}$
16	$\frac{0}{32}$	$\frac{3}{45}$	$\frac{7}{57}$	$\frac{12}{68}$	$\frac{16}{80}$	$\frac{21}{91}$	$\frac{26}{102}$	$\frac{31}{113}$	$\frac{36}{124}$
17	$\frac{0}{34}$	$\frac{4}{47}$	$\frac{8}{60}$	$\frac{13}{72}$	$\frac{18}{84}$	$\frac{23}{96}$	$\frac{28}{108}$	$\frac{33}{120}$	$\frac{38}{132}$
18	$\frac{0}{36}$	$\frac{4}{50}$	$\frac{9}{63}$	$\frac{14}{76}$	$\frac{19}{89}$	$\frac{24}{102}$	$\frac{30}{114}$	$\frac{36}{126}$	$\frac{41}{139}$
19	$\frac{1}{37}$	$\frac{4}{53}$	$\frac{9}{67}$	$\frac{15}{80}$	$\frac{20}{94}$	$\frac{26}{107}$	$\frac{32}{120}$	$\frac{38}{133}$	$\frac{44}{146}$
20	$\frac{1}{39}$	$\frac{5}{55}$	$\frac{10}{70}$	$\frac{16}{84}$	$\frac{22}{98}$	$\frac{28}{112}$	$\frac{34}{126}$	$\frac{40}{140}$	$\frac{47}{153}$

Dashes in the table indicate that no decision is possible at the stated level of significance. When either n_1 or n_2 is one, the test is not possible.

(Adapted from Tables J and K, Siegel, S. 1956. *Nonparametric statistics for the behavioural sciences*, McGraw-Hill)

Appendix E (*cont.*)
Mann–Whitney U test (significance level of 0.01, one-tailed test)

11	12	13	14	15	16	17	18	19	20
–	–	0/26	0/28	0/30	0/32	0/34	0/36	1/37	1/39
1/32	2/34	2/37	2/40	3/42	3/45	4/47	4/50	4/52	5/55
4/40	5/43	5/47	6/50	7/53	7/57	8/60	9/63	9/67	10/70
7/48	8/52	9/56	10/60	11/64	12/68	13/72	14/76	15/80	16/84
9/57	11/61	12/66	13/71	15/75	16/80	18/84	19/89	20/94	22/98
12/65	14/70	16/75	17/81	19/86	21/91	23/96	24/102	26/107	28/112
15/73	17/79	20/84	22/90	24/96	26/102	28/108	30/114	32/120	34/126
18/81	21/87	23/94	26/100	28/107	31/113	33/120	36/126	38/133	40/140
22/88	24/96	27/103	30/110	33/117	36/124	38/132	41/139	44/146	47/153
25/96	28/104	31/112	34/120	37/128	41/135	44/143	47/151	50/159	53/167
28/104	31/113	35/121	38/130	42/138	46/146	49/155	53/163	56/172	60/180
31/112	35/121	39/130	43/139	47/148	51/157	55/166	59/175	63/184	67/193
34/120	38/130	43/139	47/149	51/159	56/168	60/178	65/187	69/197	73/207
37/128	42/138	47/148	51/159	56/169	61/179	66/189	70/200	75/210	80/220
41/135	46/146	51/157	56/168	61/179	66/190	71/201	76/212	82/222	87/233
44/143	49/155	55/166	60/178	66/189	71/201	77/212	82/224	88/234	93/247
47/151	53/163	59/175	65/187	70/200	76/212	82/224	88/236	94/248	100/260
50/159	56/172	63/184	69/197	75/210	82/222	88/235	94/248	101/260	107/273
53/167	60/180	67/193	73/207	80/220	87/233	93/247	100/260	107/273	114/286

Appendix F

Critical values of T in the Wilcoxon Matched Pairs test

N	Significance level of 5% (one-tailed test)	Significance level of 5% (two-tailed test)	Significance level of 1% (one-tailed test)	Significance level of 1% (two-tailed test)
6	2 19	0 21		
7	3 25	2 26	0 28	
8	5 31	3 33	1 35	0 36
9	8 37	5 40	3 42	1 44
10	10 45	8 47	5 50	3 52
11	13 53	10 56	7 59	5 61
12	17 61	13 65	9 69	7 71
13	21 70	17 74	12 79	9 82
14	25 80	21 84	15 90	12 93
15	30 90	25 95	19 101	15 105
16	35 101	29 107	23 113	19 117
17	41 112	34 119	27 126	23 130
18	47 124	40 131	32 139	27 144
19	53 137	46 144	37 153	32 158
20	60 150	52 158	43 167	37 173
21	67 164	58 173	49 182	42 189
22	75 178	65 188	55 198	48 205
23	83 193	73 203	62 214	54 222
24	91 209	81 219	69 231	61 239
25	100 225	89 236	76 249	68 257

(Adapted from Table G. Siegel S. 1956. *Nonparametric statistics for the behavioural sciences,* McGraw-Hill)

Appendix G

Critical values of F (variance ratio)
Significance levels of 0.05 (top row) and 0.01 (bottom row)

		1	2	3	4	5	6	7	8	9
Degrees of freedom for greater standard deviation square										
	1	161	200	216	225	230	234	237	239	241
		4052	4999	5403	5625	5764	5859	5928	5981	6022
	2	18.51	19.00	19.16	19.25	19.30	19.33	19.36	19.37	19.38
		98.49	99.01	99.17	99.25	99.30	99.33	99.34	99.36	99.38
	3	10.13	9.55	9.28	9.12	9.01	8.94	8.88	8.84	8.81
		34.12	30.81	29.46	28.71	28.24	27.91	27.67	27.49	27.34
	4	7.71	6.94	6.59	6.39	6.26	6.16	6.09	6.04	6.00
		21.20	18.00	16.69	15.98	15.52	15.21	14.98	14.80	14.66
Degrees of freedom for lesser standard deviation square	5	6.61	5.79	5.41	5.19	5.05	4.95	4.88	4.82	4.78
		16.26	13.27	12.06	11.39	10.97	10.67	10.45	10.27	10.15
	6	5.99	5.14	4.76	4.53	4.39	4.28	4.21	4.15	4.10
		13.74	10.92	9.78	9.15	8.75	8.47	8.26	8.10	7.98
	7	5.59	4.74	4.35	4.12	3.97	3.87	3.79	3.73	3.68
		12.25	9.55	8.45	7.85	7.46	7.19	7.00	6.84	6.71
	8	5.32	4.46	4.07	3.84	3.69	3.58	3.50	3.44	3.39
		11.26	8.65	7.59	7.01	6.63	6.37	6.19	6.03	5.91
	9	5.12	4.26	3.86	3.63	3.48	3.37	3.29	3.23	3.18
		10.56	8.02	6.99	6.42	6.06	5.80	5.62	5.47	5.35
	10	4.96	4.10	3.71	3.48	3.33	3.22	3.14	3.07	3.02
		10.04	7.56	6.55	5.99	5.64	5.39	5.21	5.06	4.95
	11	4.84	3.98	3.59	3.36	3.20	3.09	3.01	2.95	2.90
		9.65	7.20	6.22	5.67	5.32	5.07	4.88	4.74	4.63
	12	4.75	3.88	3.49	3.26	3.11	3.00	2.92	2.85	2.80
		9.33	6.93	5.95	5.41	5.06	4.82	4.65	4.50	4.39
	13	4.67	3.80	3.41	3.18	3.02	2.92	2.84	2.77	2.72
		9.07	6.70	5.74	5.20	4.86	4.62	4.44	4.30	4.19
	14	4.60	3.74	3.34	3.11	2.96	2.85	2.77	2.70	2.65
		8.86	6.51	5.56	5.03	4.69	4.46	4.28	4.14	4.03
	15	4.54	3.68	3.29	3.06	2.90	2.79	2.70	2.64	2.59
		8.68	6.36	5.42	4.89	4.56	4.32	4.14	4.00	3.89

Appendix G (*cont.*)
Critical values of F (variance ratio)
Significance levels of 0.05 (top row) and 0.01 (bottom row)

Degrees of freedom for greater standard deviation square

10	11	12	14	16	20	24	50	100	200	∞
242	243	244	245	246	248	249	252	253	254	254
6056	6082	6106	6142	6169	6208	6234	6302	6334	6352	6366
19.39	19.40	19.41	19.42	19.43	19.44	19.45	19.47	19.49	19.49	19.50
99.40	99.41	99.42	99.43	99.44	99.45	99.46	99.48	99.49	99.49	99.50
8.78	8.76	8.74	8.71	8.69	8.66	8.64	8.58	8.56	8.54	8.53
27.23	27.13	27.05	26.92	26.83	26.69	26.60	26.30	26.23	26.18	26.12
5.96	5.93	5.91	5.87	5.84	5.80	5.77	5.70	5.66	5.65	5.63
14.54	14.45	14.37	14.24	14.15	14.02	13.93	13.69	13.57	13.52	13.46
4.74	4.70	4.68	4.64	4.60	4.56	4.53	4.44	4.40	4.38	4.36
10.05	9.96	9.89	9.77	9.48	9.55	9.47	9.24	9.13	9.07	9.02
4.06	4.03	4.00	3.96	3.92	3.87	3.84	3.75	3.71	3.69	3.67
7.87	7.79	7.72	7.60	7.52	7.39	7.31	7.09	6.99	6.94	6.88
3.63	3.60	3.57	3.52	3.49	3.44	3.41	3.32	3.28	3.25	3.23
6.62	6.54	6.47	6.35	6.27	6.15	6.07	5.85	5.75	5.70	5.65
3.34	3.31	3.28	3.23	3.20	3.15	3.12	3.03	2.98	2.96	2.93
5.82	5.74	5.67	5.56	5.48	5.36	5.28	5.06	4.96	4.91	4.86
3.13	3.10	3.07	3.02	2.98	2.93	2.90	2.80	2.76	2.73	2.71
5.26	5.18	5.11	5.00	4.92	4.80	4.73	4.51	4.41	4.36	4.31
2.97	2.94	2.91	2.86	2.82	2.77	2.74	2.64	2.59	2.56	2.54
4.85	4.78	4.71	4.60	4.52	4.41	4.33	4.12	4.01	3.96	3.91
2.86	2.82	2.79	2.74	2.70	2.65	2.61	2.50	2.45	2.42	2.40
4.54	4.46	4.40	4.29	4.21	4.10	4.02	3.80	3.70	3.66	3.60
2.76	2.72	2.69	2.64	2.60	2.54	2.50	2.40	2.35	2.32	2.30
4.30	4.22	4.16	4.05	3.98	3.86	3.78	3.56	3.46	3.41	3.36
2.67	2.63	2.60	2.55	2.51	2.46	2.42	2.32	2.26	2.24	2.21
4.10	4.02	3.96	3.85	3.78	3.67	3.59	3.37	3.27	3.21	3.16
2.60	2.56	2.53	2.48	2.44	2.39	2.35	2.24	2.19	2.16	2.13
3.94	3.86	3.80	3.70	3.62	3.51	3.43	3.21	3.11	3.06	3.00
2.55	2.51	2.48	2.43	2.39	2.33	2.29	2.18	2.12	2.10	2.07
3.73	3.73	3.67	3.56	3.48	3.36	3.29	3.07	2.97	2.92	2.87

Appendix G (*cont.*)
Critical values of F (variance ratio)
Significance levels of 0.05 (top row) and 0.01 (bottom row)

Degrees of freedom for greater standard deviation square

	1	2	3	4	5	6	7	8	9
16	4.49	3.63	3.24	3.01	2.85	2.74	2.66	2.59	2.54
	8.53	6.23	5.29	4.77	4.44	4.20	4.03	3.89	3.78
17	4.45	3.59	3.20	2.96	2.81	2.70	2.62	2.55	2.50
	8.40	6.11	5.18	4.67	4.34	4.10	3.93	3.79	3.68
18	4.41	3.55	3.16	2.93	2.77	2.66	2.58	2.51	2.56
	8.28	6.01	5.09	4.58	4.25	4.01	3.85	3.71	3.60
19	4.38	3.52	3.13	2.90	2.74	2.63	2.55	2.48	2.43
	8.18	5.93	5.01	4.50	4.17	3.94	3.77	3.62	3.52
20	4.35	3.49	3.10	2.87	2.71	2.60	2.52	2.45	2.40
	8.10	5.85	4.94	4.43	4.10	3.87	3.71	3.56	3.45
21	4.32	3.47	3.07	2.84	2.68	2.57	2.49	2.42	2.37
	8.02	5.78	4.87	4.37	4.04	3.81	3.65	3.51	3.40
22	4.30	3.44	3.05	2.82	2.66	2.55	2.47	2.40	2.35
	7.96	5.72	4.82	4.31	3.99	3.76	3.59	3.45	3.35
23	4.28	3.42	3.03	2.80	2.64	2.53	2.45	2.38	2.32
	7.88	5.66	4.76	4.26	3.94	3.71	3.54	3.41	3.30
24	4.26	3.40	3.01	2.78	2.62	2.51	2.43	2.36	2.30
	7.82	5.61	4.72	4.22	3.90	3.67	3.50	3.36	3.25
25	4.24	3.38	2.99	2.76	2.60	2.49	2.41	2.34	2.28
	7.77	5.57	4.68	4.18	3.86	3.63	3.46	3.32	3.21
26	4.22	3.37	2.89	2.74	2.59	2.47	2.39	2.32	2.27
	7.72	5.53	4.64	4.14	3.82	3.59	3.42	3.29	3.17
27	4.21	3.35	2.96	2.73	2.57	2.46	2.37	2.30	2.25
	7.68	5.49	4.60	4.11	3.79	3.56	3.39	3.26	3.14
28	4.20	3.34	2.95	2.71	2.56	2.44	2.36	2.29	2.24
	7.66	5.45	4.57	4.07	3.76	3.53	3.36	3.23	3.11
29	4.18	3.33	2.93	2.70	2.54	2.43	2.35	2.28	2.22
	7.60	5.52	4.54	4.04	3.73	3.50	3.32	3.20	3.08
30	4.17	3.32	2.92	2.69	2.53	2.42	2.34	2.27	2.21
	7.56	5.39	4.51	4.02	3.70	3.47	3.30	3.17	3.06

Degrees of freedom for lesser standard deviation square

Appendix G (*cont.*)
Critical values of F (variance ratio)
Significance levels of 0.05 (top row) and 0.01 (bottom row)

Degrees of freedom for greater standard deviation square

10	11	12	14	16	20	24	50	100	200	∞
2.49	2.45	2.42	2.37	2.33	2.28	2.24	2.13	2.07	2.04	2.01
3.69	3.61	3.55	3.45	3.37	3.25	3.18	2.96	2.86	2.80	2.75
2.45	2.41	2.38	2.33	2.29	2.23	2.19	2.08	2.02	1.99	1.96
3.59	3.52	3.45	3.35	3.27	3.16	3.08	2.86	2.76	2.70	2.65
2.41	2.37	2.34	2.29	2.25	2.19	2.15	2.04	1.98	1.95	1.92
3.51	3.44	3.37	3.27	3.19	3.07	3.00	2.78	2.68	2.62	2.57
2.38	2.34	2.31	2.26	2.21	2.15	2.11	2.00	1.94	1.91	1.88
3.43	3.36	3.30	3.19	3.12	3.00	2.92	2.70	2.60	2.54	2.49
2.35	2.31	2.28	2.23	2.18	2.12	2.08	1.96	1.90	1.87	1.84
3.37	3.30	3.23	3.13	3.05	2.94	2.86	2.63	2.53	2.47	2.42
2.32	2.28	2.25	2.20	2.15	2.09	2.05	1.93	1.87	1.84	1.81
3.31	3.24	3.17	3.07	2.99	2.88	2.80	2.58	2.47	2.42	2.36
2.30	2.26	2.23	2.18	2.13	2.07	2.03	1.91	1.84	1.81	1.78
3.26	3.18	3.12	3.02	2.94	2.83	2.75	2.53	2.42	2.37	2.31
2.28	2.24	2.20	2.14	2.10	2.04	2.00	1.88	1.82	1.79	1.76
3.21	3.14	3.07	2.97	2.89	2.78	2.70	2.48	2.37	2.32	2.26
2.26	2.22	2.18	2.13	2.09	2.02	1.98	1.86	1.80	1.76	1.73
3.17	3.09	3.03	2.93	2.85	2.74	2.66	2.44	2.33	2.27	2.21
2.24	2.20	2.16	2.11	2.06	2.00	1.96	1.84	1.77	1.74	1.71
3.13	3.05	2.99	2.89	2.81	2.70	2.62	2.40	2.29	2.23	2.17
2.22	2.18	2.15	2.10	2.05	1.99	1.95	1.82	1.76	1.72	1.69
3.09	3.02	2.96	2.86	2.77	2.66	2.58	2.36	2.25	2.19	2.13
2.20	2.16	2.13	2.08	2.03	1.97	1.93	1.80	1.74	1.71	1.67
3.06	2.98	2.93	2.83	2.74	2.63	2.55	2.33	2.21	2.16	2.10
2.19	2.15	2.12	2.06	2.02	1.96	1.91	1.78	1.72	1.69	1.65
3.03	2.95	2.90	2.80	2.71	2.60	1.52	2.30	2.18	2.13	2.06
2.18	2.14	2.10	2.05	2.00	1.94	1.90	1.77	1.71	1.68	1.64
3.00	2.92	2.87	2.77	2.68	2.57	2.49	2.27	2.15	2.10	2.03
2.16	2.12	2.09	2.04	1.99	1.93	1.89	1.76	1.69	1.66	1.62
2.98	2.90	2.84	2.74	2.66	2.55	2.47	2.24	2.13	2.07	2.01

Appendix G (*cont.*)

Critical values of F (variance ratio)

Significance levels of 0.05 (top row) and 0.01 (bottom row)

		1	2	3	4	5	6	7	8	9
		\multicolumn{9}{c}{*Degrees of freedom for greater standard deviation square*}								
	40	4.08	3.23	2.84	2.61	2.45	2.34	2.25	2.18	2.12
		7.31	5.18	4.31	3.83	3.51	3.29	3.12	2.99	2.88
	50	4.03	3.18	2.79	2.56	2.40	2.29	2.20	2.13	2.07
		7.17	5.06	4.20	3.72	3.41	3.18	3.02	2.88	2.78
	60	4.00	3.15	2.76	2.52	2.37	2.25	2.17	2.10	2.04
		7.08	4.98	4.13	3.65	3.34	3.12	2.95	2.82	2.72
	100	3.94	3.09	2.70	2.46	2.30	2.19	2.10	2.03	1.97
		6.90	4.82	3.98	3.51	3.20	2.99	2.82	2.69	2.59
	200	3.89	3.04	2.65	2.41	2.26	2.14	2.05	1.98	1.92
		6.76	4.71	3.38	3.41	3.11	2.90	2.73	2.60	2.50
	∞	3.84	2.99	2.60	2.37	2.21	2.09	2.01	1.94	1.88
		6.64	4.60	3.78	3.32	3.02	2.80	2.64	2.51	2.41

Degrees of freedom for lesser standard deviation square

(Adapted from Table V, Fisher, R.A. and Yates, F. 1963. *Statistical tables for biological, agricultural and medical research*, 6th edn, Oliver & Boyd)

Appendix G (*cont.*)
Critical values of F (variance ratio)
Significance levels of 0.05 (top row) and 0.01 (bottom row)

Degrees of freedom for greater standard deviation square

10	11	12	14	16	20	24	50	100	200	∞
2.07	2.04	2.00	1.95	1.90	1.84	1.79	1.66	1.59	1.55	1.51
2.80	2.73	2.66	2.56	2.49	2.37	2.29	2.05	1.94	1.88	1.81
2.02	1.98	1.95	1.90	1.85	1.78	1.74	1.60	1.52	1.48	1.44
2.70	2.62	2.56	2.46	2.39	2.26	2.18	1.94	1.82	1.76	1.68
1.99	1.95	1.92	1.86	1.81	1.75	1.70	1.56	1.48	1.44	1.39
2.63	2.56	2.50	2.40	2.32	2.20	2.12	1.87	1.74	1.68	1.60
1.92	1.88	1.85	1.79	1.75	1.68	1.63	1.48	1.39	1.34	1.28
2.51	2.43	2.36	2.26	2.19	2.06	1.98	1.73	1.59	1.51	1.43
1.87	1.83	1.80	1.74	1.69	1.62	1.57	1.42	1.32	1.26	1.19
2.41	2.34	2.28	2.17	2.09	1.97	1.88	1.62	1.48	1.39	1.28
1.83	1.79	1.75	1.69	1.64	1.57	1.52	1.35	1.24	1.17	1.00
2.32	2.24	2.18	2.07	1.99	1.87	1.79	1.52	1.36	1.25	1.00

Appendix H
Critical values of t (Student's test)

Degrees of freedom	Significance level of 0.05 (one-tailed)	Significance level of 0.05 (two-tailed)	Significance level of 0.01 (one-tailed)	Significance level of 0.01 (two-tailed)
1	6.31	12.71	31.82	63.66
2	2.92	4.30	6.97	9.93
3	2.35	3.18	4.54	5.84
4	2.13	2.78	3.75	4.60
5	2.02	2.57	3.37	4.03
6	1.94	2.45	3.14	3.71
7	1.90	2.37	3.00	3.50
8	1.86	2.31	2.90	3.36
9	1.83	2.26	2.82	3.25
10	1.81	2.23	2.76	3.17
11	1.80	2.20	2.72	3.11
12	1.78	2.18	2.68	3.06
13	1.77	2.16	2.65	3.01
14	1.76	2.15	2.62	2.98
15	1.75	2.13	2.60	2.95
16	1.75	2.12	2.58	2.92
17	1.74	2.11	2.57	2.90
18	1.73	2.10	2.55	2.88
19	1.73	2.09	2.54	2.86
20	1.73	2.09	2.53	2.85
21	1.72	2.08	2.52	2.83
22	1.72	2.07	2.51	2.82
23	1.71	2.07	2.50	2.81
24	1.71	2.06	2.49	2.80
25	1.70	2.06	2.49	2.79
26	1.71	2.06	2.48	2.78
27	1.70	2.05	2.47	2.77
28	1.70	2.05	2.47	2.76
29	1.70	2.05	2.46	2.76
30	1.70	2.04	2.46	2.75
40	1.68	2.02	2.42	2.70
60	1.67	2.00	2.39	2.66
120	1.66	1.98	2.36	2.62
∞	1.65	1.96	2.33	2.58

(Adapted from Table III, Fisher, R.A. and Yates, F. 1963. *Statistical tables for biological, agricultural and medical research*, 6th edn, Oliver & Boyd)

Index